UNIVERSAL DESIGN

Oliver Herwig

UNIVERSAL DESIGN

Solutions for a barrier-free living

Birkhäuser
Basel · Boston · Berlin

CONTENTS

My Five Hypotheses

First hypothesis: Tomorrow's society will be older, more varied, and more difficult to narrow down to a consensus.

Second hypothesis: The future will not be won with more equipment and more intelligent features, but with products that make life easier.

Third hypothesis: There will be a fundamental shift in perspectives. We will not develop a more aerodynamic Rollator, but rather build houses and spaces that are accessible for all.

Fourth hypothesis: The balance shifts the moment the new seniors stop standing in line at the pharmacy holding a prescription, and begin working as salespeople in department stores. Demand creates new products, and choice creates the market.

Fifth hypothesis: Studying seniors leads to better designs.

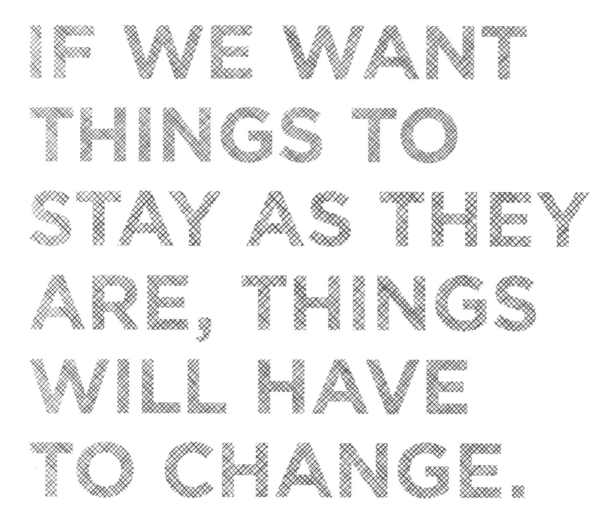

IF WE WANT
THINGS TO
STAY AS THEY
ARE, THINGS
WILL HAVE
TO CHANGE.

GIUSEPPE TOMASI DI LAMPEDUSA, *THE LEOPARD*

UNIVERSAL DESIGN MEANS DESIGN FOR EVERYONE

This book was written from a central European perspective. Initially, I only planned to write about objects and rooms for seniors, but I then realized that it is not a matter of targeted solutions. It concerns us all. It is about Universal Design.

The book would have come to different conclusions had it been about Japan, or the United States or Russia. Because societies think, feel, and age differently. However there are certain things such as desires, ambitions, and dreams that remain consistent. Some are addressed here. Yet this book should not exhaust itself completely on things and spaces, but rather offer perspectives on and open horizons to a new, barrier-free world for everyone. In this sense, Universal Design is a key.

There are two very different kinds of forecasts: hard and soft. Those that quote numbers seem to be correct, but those that make general predictions cannot be disputed. I would like to move between both poles and formulate five hypotheses.

First: Tomorrow's society will be older, more varied, and more difficult to trim down to a consensus.

How does that feel? To answer this, it is worth recalling the last century's view of the future. A car that ran on atomic power did not seem impossible or even dangerous; it was inevitable. The Ford Nucleon was designed to travel up to 8,000 kilometers.

The nuclear reactor beneath the extended front did not even change the car's design very much. In 1957, it even became feasible to have a car without a driver. It was designed to travel along rails above an empty highway while inside the family played a board game: a timeless vision betrayed only by the characteristic tail fins on the car and the occupants' ideal family clothing and hairstyles. It is a view of the 1950s but also one of the future. Driverless cars have long been in use and will be traveling along our streets in a few years. Unbelievable.

We have relinquished the steering wheel, but the nuclear car proved a technical dead end that belongs to the past. What the future will look like is still unclear, but not the powers that fuel it.

Population statistics are a fact and thus have little to do with inventions and technology. In 2030, my generation, those in their forties today, will be the relative majority. Maybe we will plot a conspiracy of elders, or be lying in a hospital, sedated and with no one to care for us because we

Nuvo
Japanese Service Robot,
manufactured by ZMP Inc.

There is no other nation more enamored
with robots and progress than Japan.
Will automatic household maids also take
on the service work here? Would they
entertain and care for the old and frail?
The idea alone makes some people's
blood run cold.

had far too few children. The nice robot nurse envisaged by the Japanese will certainly not be at our bedside.

This leads me to my second hypothesis: The future will not be won with more equipment and more intelligent features, but with products that make life easier. Perhaps you are thinking about walking sticks, wheelchairs, or so-called monkey poles. But I am not. Medical supplies design will remain a specialized niche, even in the future.

I am speaking about the real possibility of over-aging, the possibility of perhaps the most critical and wealthiest social stratum exacting new standards that will be simplified, clearer, and more helpful.

I am speaking of things not tailored only toward a specific target group, that is, either hipsters in their mid-twenties or the senile elderly, I am thinking about how the change that is gaining momentum in our society demands and supports a new understanding of design.

Universal products will exist again for the first time since Henry Ford exhibited the process of mass production to the public — things that merge aesthetics, ergonomics, comfort, and cool lines. They are classy and forgive the odd operational error. If I can no longer operate the keyboard, I'll switch the computer to speech mode. Or use my finger on the monitor.

Age provides an opportunity for anyone addressing the issue as a designer — but also for politicians. The small comes to the great. And now for my third hypothesis: Perspectives will shift fundamentally. We will not develop a more aerodynamic Rollator, but rather build houses and spaces that are accessible to all. The house will no longer be a rigid fortress, but rather a temporary, convertable structure that adapts to singles, families, and seniors. Apartments will grow and shrink in size again if the extra space can no longer be supported. Generation houses that expand: the grandparents move upstairs into the extension above the carport, the family live downstairs, and when the children are grown they can exchange places with their elders.

Intuitive objects are added to the flexible rooms. We will immediately sense how to operate a product, and no longer get lost in a jungle of control menus. Let's call it the television principle. Turn it on, choose a program, lean back and enjoy. If technology develops in three steps, primitive — complex — simple, then the last step is still missing.

The senior market is a growth market. Japan recognized this a long time ago. The Far East is at least ten years ahead of us. METI, the all-powerful Ministry for Economy, Trade and Industry, recognized the senior economy long ago as a driving force and circulated the motto about "changing population aging into a growth machine." From Panasonic to the cosmetic giants, seniors are respected as valuable customers worth attracting by means of product innovations and product campaigns. This is based on an awareness that is more advanced than most western societies. Japan tackles the challenge of aging in such a way that the amenities of a low-barrier or even barrier-free environment and new, intuitively operable, simple appliances can be a benefit to all. The resonant prejudice that we harbor toward senior-friendly, or in other words "senile," products does not exist. This development is very real and tangible. For a good ten years, Japan has been producing so-called *Kyôyo hin* products, or "universally usable" goods that fulfill all the requirements of Universal Design and thus pervade and alter everyday life as a whole.

Youth Commodities and Elderly Products

How does it look here? We are also getting older. Our life expectancy increases by an average of three months a year. This is hardly a gentle rise but more of a bounce, encouraging researchers to predict that celebrating a 100th birthday in the twenty-second century will be a normal occurrence. In addition to this, people remain healthy longer, according to a study by scientists at the Max Planck Institute for Demographic Research in Rostock. [1] The much praised consumer society admittedly turns flaccid when it comes to the age issue. Our youth craze only produces youth commodities. There is no room for universal things, no market, no target group. This has to change as quickly as possible, because nothing is growing as fast as the percentage of seniors. In 2030 the over-sixty generation will comprise one third of the German population, and according to some statisticians, one half. The future seniors will definitely not be a generation of feeble old-timers, nor will they wish to deal with the perils of day-to-day life and its objects: with tiny print, elegantly hidden pushbuttons, confusing multifunctional appliances, or cars with doors designed more for Michael Schumacher's descendants. Where are the coffee machines for the over-sixty generation, or the

1   *Hundert wird bald jeder* (Soon we will all reach 100). Max Planck Society press release, September 27, 2007. http://www.mpg.de/bilderBerichteDokumente/dokumentation/pressemitteilungen/2007/pressemitteilung200709272/genPDF.pdf

Interieur
Designed by 03 Architects

How can tomorrow's spaces be made to function for everyone? The wheelchair-adapted table is still a luxury, but in the future such insightful planning will become the norm. Wheelchair-accessible apartments and houses are what lie ahead.

iPod with the easy-to-use click wheel? They will come. The good things for retirement. And they will not be hidden in medical and home care supplies stores; you will find them in shop around the corner, or on the first page of the mail-order catalog. Because the self-styled silver surfers have money and they will soon dominate the market. The consumer quota, meaning what is spent in relation to available earnings, begins to increase in our mid-forties, and by the time we are in our mid-sixties and mid-seventies, has reached its maximum of eighty-four percent. "The so-called old-timers want to consume, and they possess more market power than the supposedly consumption-obsessed mid-twenty, mid-thirty, and mid-forty generations targeted almost exclusively by the advertising industry for decades.

Fifty percent of all German new cars are bought by people who are over fifty, and at the luxury level, this rises to eighty percent; the over-fifty generation also buy fifty-five percent of all coffee, fifty percent of all facial care products, fifty percent of mineral water, and eighty percent

WMF1

Coffee Pad Machine by designafairs

This is the smallest coffee pad machine in the world, boasts WMF, clear and concise in form and easy to use. Fill it up, position the cup, and push the button. This development earned the designers at designafairs in Munich the "Universal Design" quality seal.

of all cruise journeys. They travel more and for longer periods of time than their younger counterparts, and stay more often in hotels. They drink more sherry and brandy and play more lotto," [2] writes Stefan Scheytt in *brand eins*: "Getting older is fun. Getting older is sexy, because getting older means: let's spend money."

2 Scheytt, Stefan: "Woopies. Sie haben Geld. Sie haben Zeit. Und alte Menschen können noch eine Menge brauchen." (Whoopies. They have money. They have time. And seniors need a lot of things.) *brand eins* 9/2005. http://www.brand-eins.de/ximages/24315_100diealte.pdf *

But rather than broadening or even altering their product ranges, industry is still playing a shameful game of hide and seek. Porsche, however, equipped its Cayenne SUV with extra wide doors, a higher access level and back-friendly seats — and thus inadvertently created the first "senior-friendly Porsche." It sounds like a term of abuse, or at best a joke. Watch out: old people! Social change is obviously a dimension that has not yet entered the minds of mainstream advertising, which still prefers to portray its target groups sitting on Harleys or wearing miniskirts, rather than the average consumer of advancing age. "A major obstacle to developing marketing strategies" for new products is "the age difference between the target groups and the mainly very young product developers and marketing experts," complains the Deutsche Bank Research in its July 2003 dossier. And it reaches a sobering conclusion: "Aging customers are a challenge to business on all levels."

The majority of companies either react "hesitantly or simply do nothing. Many openly fear destroying their hard-won 'young image'." And this can be confirmed by anyone wanting to purchase a senior-friendly or arthritis-compatible product, such as a radio for instance. It is an absurd experience. Just go to the games department, the busy salesperson will tell you. My first Sony is now suddenly my last. Colorful, gaudy, with huge buttons and handles. For a half a century you have lived with well-designed artifacts only now to be degraded to a child.

But it could be different. Simplephone is the name of a mobile telephone developed in Holland — just a phone with large buttons and no complicated control menus. The softly rounded mobile has an illuminated display that is easy to read, large numbers, equally large buttons, and an adjustable speaker function. Even the Swedes are more advanced. Ergon, the ergonomically angled bread knife, is helpful for those with arthritic joints and can even be purchased at IKEA. At last this shows that there is no need for special senior-friendly products, only for well-designed products. Yet a cultural change is first needed in order to overcome the stigma of age and its supportive aids, and to provide very normal products for day-to-day problem solving.

This leads to my fourth hypothesis: The balance shifts the moment the new seniors stop standing in line at the pharmacy holding a prescription, and begin working as salespersons in department stores. Demand creates new products, and choice creates the market.

The thesis work of Diana Kraus displays the potential elegance of senior-friendly design. Together with Miele, she created the fifty-plus kitchen concept, a type of twenty-first-century Frankfurt kitchen without the charm of a laboratory. You are meant to live in this kitchen, to relax and keep in touch with the environment. The design goes below the surface of flowing lines and clear materials. There is a deeper dimension of practical details, such as the adjustable water faucet. It can be brought in an energy-saving manner to the pot, and not the other way round.

This brings me to my last hypothesis: Studying seniors leads to better designs. Because seniors are the toughest testers. If they are happy with a product everyone else will be too. This applies to products used in everyday life as well as to Internet design. Web designers love tiny print, almost tone on tone against a monochrome background, meaning beige on a light brown background or dark gray on light gray. And because it is so cool and aesthetic, most people cannot read it without an electric magnifying glass. But that too will change. What will look old in the future is typeface that is not at least twelve-point in size and not set on a background with enough contrast. The attractive new world of tomorrow will be clearer, simpler, safer. And everyone will benefit from it. Barrier-free houses and objects are a massive step forward. The geriatric generation of 2046 will demand both function and beauty. Its design should be in the position to finally fulfill the greatest promise of Modernism. Ergonomics and good looks in one. And that is a prognosis, as soft or as hard as may be. We first need to overcome the barriers in our heads, then those in our environment. Comfort will be the key which allows an entire generation of new products to soon capture our day-to-day lives.

Arriving at the "Quality of Life" — Terminology

Designing for everyone instead of discriminating against seniors. The direction is clear, but not the terminology. A lively chaos of terms still presides with subtle efforts to differentiate and define, as is typical for a relatively new field. Three main terms often accompany and sometimes contradict one another: Universal Design, Inclusive Design, and Design for All. They are often supplemented by words such as ergonomics and usability. If the evidence can be trusted, the point is to establish a market and define different realms of interest and influence. It is unlikely that all of these terms will survive, however Universal Design is the one with the greatest chance of persevering. Introduced decades ago by Ron Mace, it became known through the Center for Universal Design at NC State University, as described in the appendix to this book: "He coined the term 'universal design' to describe the concept of designing all products and the built environment to be aesthetic and usable to the greatest extent possible by everyone, regardless of their age, ability, or status in life. He was also a devoted advocate for the rights of people with disabilities which is reflected in his work." [3]

3 A biography and valuation of Ron Mace by the Center for Universal Design can be found at: http://www.design.ncsu.edu/cud/about_us/usronmace.htm

4 www.ud-germany.de/html/ud/g/ud/universal_design_award/universaldesignaward08download.pdf

5 As stated in the press release on the Universal Design Prize for senior-friendly automobile interiors, Hannover, March 16, 2007.

Meanwhile, even the UN has anchored Universal Design in its accord on the rights of disabled peoples. It explicitly states that Universal Design "means the design of products, environments, programs and services to be usable by all people, to the greatest extent possible, without the need for adaptation or specialized design." [4] Universal Design's charm lies precisely in the fact that the rights of minorities and special groups are protected and, as the most critical testers and most demanding users, they become the door-openers for product innovation and social change that will benefit all. It stopped being a matter of special solutions for a targeted few a long time ago. The point is to make life easier for everyone: clear to follow menus, environments, and products that can be used in various ways. More and more institutions, which award prizes and distinctions that will greatly influence our future, are affiliating themselves with this definition: "Universal Design does not mean special products for a certain group of people, but rather good design for all phases and circumstances of life. The term 'Universal Design' addresses this desire and demands intelligent solutions for every area of life and all age groups." [5]

6   The Generation Research Program at the LMU Munich differentiates from the bottom to the top: *Accessibility* — it is an important goal for the whole of society, ensuring that products, services, workplaces, and environmental conditions are designed in such a way as to make them accessible for as many as possible. *Usability* — denotes the usability of a product by describing to a certain user group how effective, efficient, and satisfying defined goals can be reached. *Acceptability* — products should not define a person as disadvantaged because of their appearance (stigmatize). Products for disadvantaged groups of people should be designed in such a way as to make them acceptable to other users. *Joy of Use* — products should not only be simple to operate and free from stigma, they should also satisfy the aesthetic needs of the user. Translated from: http://www.grp.hwz.uni-muenchen.de/pages/arbeitsgruppen/usability/index.html

A terminological definition should not, however, lead to generalized concepts, especially as Universal Design forms the umbrella brand over different design strategies. Researchers from the Generation Research Program at the Ludwig Maximilian University in Munich distinguish between four levels of design with their respective user feedback as a means of attaining the goal of "quality of life" [6]: accessibility or barrier-free access is the basis; followed by usability, user-friendliness; acceptability, or freedom from stigma and market acceptance; and finally crowned by aesthetics and emotionality: joy of use.

To ensure its success, Universal Design must be attractive for everyone. It is well worth bringing together ergonomics and beauty with wide-ranging usability and the I-want-to-have-it incentive to buy. And that is exactly what will happen.

SimpliciTEA
Ceramic Teapot with Pourer Stand,
designed by Lotte Alpert

No spillage here. Thanks to the pourer
stand, even full teapots can be poured
into cups with ease. The teapot and
the stand form one unit. The elaborate
pourer stand envelops the pot like a
hand and keeps tea or coffee warm via
induction. Diodes on the side of the pot
display the temperature of its contents.

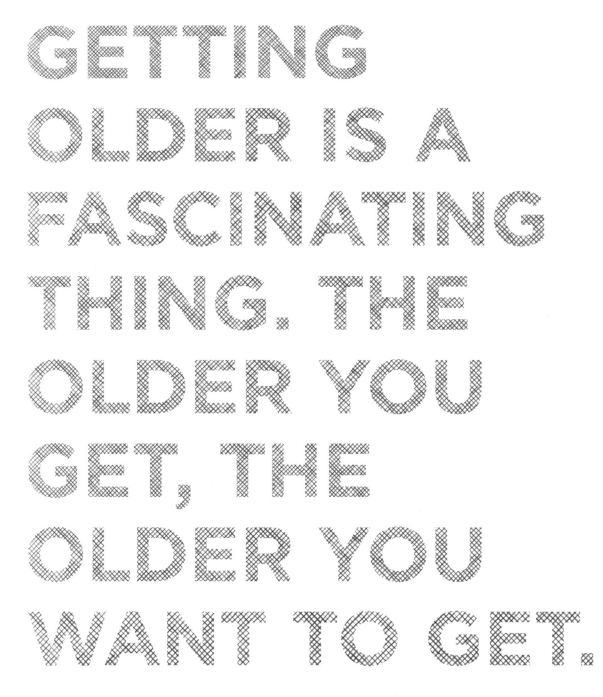

GETTING OLDER IS A FASCINATING THING. THE OLDER YOU GET, THE OLDER YOU WANT TO GET.

KEITH RICHARDS

Anything but Old — a User's Perspective

We need to recognize that old is not always old. Seniors are anything but a homogenous target group; they represent far more a collection of individual philosophies of life that become increasingly varied. Class differences fade and are replaced by individual natures. And yet there is a third, less frequently considered aspect: today's and tomorrow's seniors will develop their own rhythms and issues, especially in the United States between Sun Cities, trailer homes, and exclusive retirement residences. Nonetheless, the ever-tenacious image of bingo evenings and senior bus trips still prevails despite the fact that these represent only one segment of an increasingly diverse spectrum of active lives.

Even if sociologists make efforts to distinguish between categories and even speak of a third phase of life after education, family, and career, namely the easygoing age before real old age sets in, limits still vary from person to person: "Age is an ineffective segregation tool," warns Herbert Plischke of GRP, the Generation Research Program at Munich's Ludwig Maximilian University. Age is most importantly a process accompanied by new opportunities, challenges, and lifelong learning. The age we "feel" often varies up to fifteen years from our chronological age. This phase, which was previously seen as a period of dwindling social life and physical and intellectual autonomy, now offers new possibilities. Active seniors are the focus today. The individual.

Nevertheless, the many attempts to construct a target group out of the so-called disparities, or at least a target group corridor ranging from those who actively enjoy life to the depressed, are little more than confusing. There are many terms used by young marketing experts, such as the mature generation, the silver age, the fifty pluses or sixty pluses, the plus generation, whoopies (well-off older people), or the "cute" young at heart. Yet these say more about our society, that is, about the permanent importation of Anglo-Saxon influenced culture and values plus the incessant youth craze, than about any actual, existential orientation of older people. Is this an interesting attempt at categorization, or merely a schematic block formation that endeavors to understand the aging phenomenon? A typical example of bureaucratic systems or humorous classification? The difference is sometimes barely recognizable when, for instance, Marie-Therese Krings-Heckemeier distinguishes between four groups based on their level of domestic autonomy, [7] starting from the "young" old (aged 50—60) and ending with the "old" old (aged 80 and over).

Toelzer Dice
Music Player designed by GRP
(Generation Research Projekt)

Turn the cube and listen to music. This
is the simple principle behind the music
player originally developed for dementia
patients. There is an MP3 player inside
the 10-centimeter long, easy-to-handle
cube; speakers are located in the edges.
If the user wants to change the music,
he or she just has to turn the cube. This
intuitive principle can be easily applied
to other objects.

7 Krings-Heckemeier, Marie-Therese: *Das silberne Zeitalter — Wie wir den Wandel zu einer Gesellschaft der erweiterten Lebensspannen bewältigen können* (How we can make the shift to a society of extended life spans). Empirica, Berlin, 2007. http://www.empirica-institut.de/kufa/empi155mtk.pdf. "Group A: 'the old young' (50—60 years old): independent living and an individual style of life, improvement of quality of life with asset optimization and optimizing the location by moving house. Group B: the 'young old' (60—70 years old): a high percentage of money spent on moving (often property ownership). Group C: the 'middle old' (70—80 years old): settled in one place and senior-friendly changes in assets as well as moving into senior-friendly facilities in combination with services. Group D: the 'old old' (80 years old and over): usually 'unwilling' move into other facilities due to a need for assistance or care."

In any case, to back up the deficit hypothesis, real or perceived restrictions would not lead to a shift in design strategies toward rehabilitation and special design. On the contrary: a broad user spectrum protects against stigmatization. Let us turn the discussion around. The fact that experts have distinguished three main areas in which performance decreases during the course of one's life — optical, motor, and cognitive — should prompt designers and manufacturers to attempt to either compensate for or minimize these "deficits" via good product design. So, what might this actually mean? It could mean considering how behavior is affected when long-sightedness sets in, when depth of perception decreases and light sensitivity increases, and when the field of vision diminishes. Typography has to be legible and clearly laid out; good contrast on monitors or navigation devices is essential, while distractions such as additional windows and animated menus should be minimal. A similarly dynamic approach can be taken to (subtle) changes in motor abilities: less flexible limbs and joints, problems with balance, and diminished stability all call for an environment that is forgiving of error. Operating a mouse with trembling hands is a challenge. Here, alternative navigational methods would be beneficial, such as pull-down menus, direct links, and, above all, a clearly designed screen.

Product developers should not create new user interfaces for every new version for users whose performance is beginning to diminish, whose short-term memory is more easily disturbed by distractions, and whose attention span is generally lower. If in doubt, preexisting routines are the better and simpler option, but self-explanatory systems are without doubt the best solution. Less design is now more design.

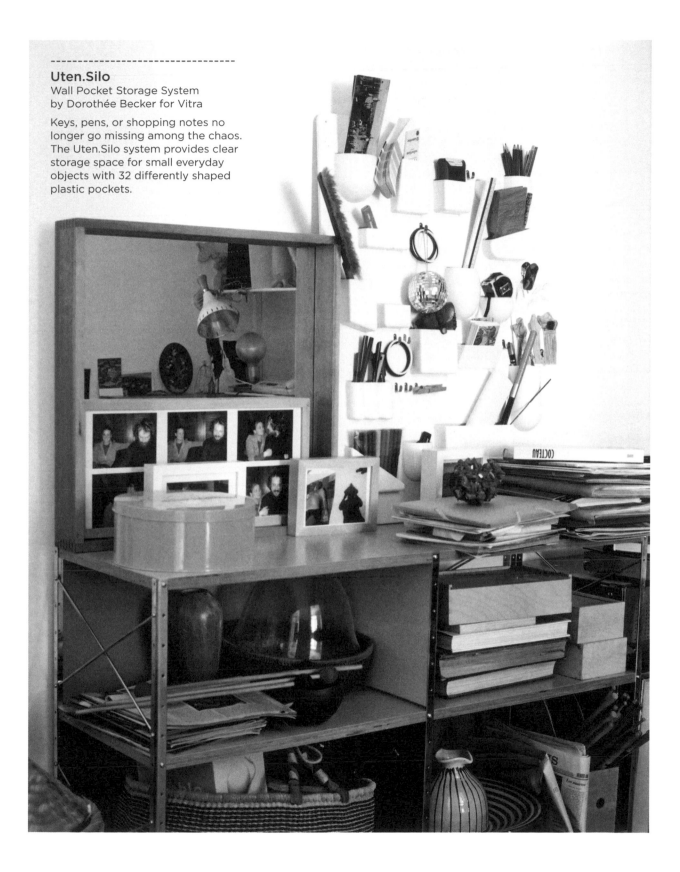

Uten.Silo
Wall Pocket Storage System
by Dorothée Becker for Vitra

Keys, pens, or shopping notes no
longer go missing among the chaos.
The Uten.Silo system provides clear
storage space for small everyday
objects with 32 differently shaped
plastic pockets.

Max and Moritz
Salt and Pepper Shakers by Wilhelm
Wagenfeld for WMF

The glass containers' slender waists
make the salt and pepper shakers set
easy to handle, but the lids do harbor
some unpleasant surprises. Users with
limited motor skills may find relief
from having to screw the lid on and off,
but if the shakers fall the lids pop off
too easily.

Vacuum Jug
Thermos Can by Erik Magnussen
for Stelton

This is the first product designed by
Erik Magnussen after inheriting Arne
Jacobsen's position as Stelton's head
designer. Today it can be seen on
conference tables across the globe.
But users have to be careful when
pouring because the thermos can's
spout is placed so high that the hot
liquid gushes out too quickly.

Observing classic design products with regard to their useful value to older or disabled people is an odd task. Because the great icons of product design, especially well-known furniture pieces, have long been considered superior to the pragmatic requirements of function and everyday necessity. Today, examples such as the "Lockheed Lounge" chaise longue by Marc Newson, tables by Zaha Hadid, and vases by Ettore Sottsass, Hella Jongerius, or Jasper Morrison are increasingly defined as works of art. At the moment, the curious expression "design art" is rather popular. It marries, as if the union were self-evident, two worlds that have long been considered incompatible: applied and fine art. Only a fool would ask if a light installation by James Turell, a sculpture by Jonathan Meese, or music by Björk would "function" for older people. Are not the colors used in many of Rembrandt's paintings so dark that people with weak vision are barely able to distinguish the fine nuances? An absurd question.

Everyday objects must of course fulfill certain functions — even those whose formal qualities have turned them into classics. Yet when it comes to classics that have been ascribed the functionless attribute of "timelessness," and which remain with their owners for decades, the question of how functional they are for older people might well have some merit.

Now the term "design classic" is neither copyrighted nor is it particularly well defined. Nonetheless, it is widely used today and very popular in the advertising context. But just because a product has been on the market for a long time does not make it a classic.

Konstantin Grcic's designs such as "Chair_ONE" (2003) or the "Myto" chair (2007), on the other hand, are sure to become classics within a few years. Yet not all the famous pieces of furniture, electronic devices, and household appliances that have been successful on the market are tailored for the special requirements of the people profiled in this book. A closer look at the superbly designed "Max and Moritz" salt and pepper shakers, created by Bauhaus designer Wilhelm Wagenfeld for WMF, reveals that the metal lids on the glass bodies can be closed by applying just a slight amount of pressure rather than screwing. This is a welcome relief, especially for people with limited haptic ability. Yet this also exposes the weak spot in Wagenfeld's concept. If the user happens to drop Max or Moritz onto a table, plate, or floor, the lid pops open and the contents go flying. The cylindrical, radically reduced vacuum jug, designed by Erik Magnussen for Stelton in 1977, has long been a standard in museum design collections and can be seen on thousands of conference or office tables across the globe. But handling the vacuum jug is somewhat tricky, because its spout is placed so high, that tea or coffee gushes out too quickly and with too much force.

Classic chair designs should also be enjoyed with care. Stuttgart design professor Winfried Scheuer witnessed, during a visit to Achille Castiglioni's studio, how the aged designer almost fell off his very own famous "Mezzadro stool" when attempting to sit on it in front of students. And the often-copied steel tube classic "S34," designed in 1926 by Mart Stam, also harbours hidden danger. Getting up from the chair can present a challenge, because the user's belt can catch onto the back of the cantilever chair, making it latch onto the body. At least here, at worst, only the chair drops to the floor.

In 1998, the exhibition "Error Design" at Kunsthalle Krems presented everyday objects and phenomena, whose shortcomings and faults have become part and parcel of the work itself: remote control devices overloaded with tiny buttons, heat-sealed plastic packaging impossible to open without using great force, or a water kettle whose handle heats up along with the water inside. Manfred Tscheligi, professor of applied computer science at the Vienna University, writes in the exhibition catalog, "We are often oblivious to the number of ineffectual objects we are confronted with on a day-to-day basis. We have just gotten used to getting annoyed. We call on every user to demand more. To demand less annoyance, fewer faults, as well as systems that function and are designed to suit a specific purpose. It is not the number of functions that makes an object successful, but rather addressing the context of its use."

In contrast, the classics listed on the following pages are proof that well-designed objects need not always present a challenge to slightly disabled persons or the elderly. On the contrary, they are not only well designed and durable, but also function extremely well. Enzo Mari's table calendar "Timor" can be adjusted on a daily basis by a simple turn of the hand; operating the mid-size "Maglite" flashlight is child's play; and the "Lamy Scribble" by Swiss designer Hannes Wettstein sits perfectly in the hand and is equipped with an easy-to-change fat cartridge. Almost

Red Cross Cabinet

Medicine Cabinet by Thomas Ericksson
for Cappellini

The cross-shape and the strong color
of this cabinet are clear signals in an
emergency: the contents of this box
can save lives.

every model of Rimowa suitcases is so lightweight and robust, that they have become reliable and useful travel companions. The straightforward medicine cabinet, designed by Thomas Ericksson in the form of a red cross, advertises its contents to strangers in the home of an injured or unconscious person, thereby helping to provide quick assistance. The Braun "Zylindric" table lighter, designed in 1968 by Dieter Rams, is indisputably an easy-to-use classic that, regrettably, has been discontinued. Its now 76-year-old designer gave up smoking years ago and keeps himself in shape by hiking, skiing, and swimming — and he is unquestionably in very good shape.

Lamy Scribble
Pen by Hannes Wettstein

The pen is easy for anyone to hold thanks to the rounded shape of its plastic casing.

Maglite
Flashlight by Anthony Maglica

It provides the light in dark situations. The Maglite flashlight is simple to use and extremely lightweight due to its aluminum casing.

Timor

Table Calendar by Enzo Mari for Danese

Turn it once to start a new day. Previous
days and months disappear into the foot
of the table calendar. The easy-to-read
letters and the clear form are both timeless and functional.

On Using the Users' Perspective

Mathias Knigge maintains that aging is part of a process, not a problem. Mechanical engineers and designers do not consider the senior-friendly environment as a task for future designers, but rather a very personal mission. Knigge has been studying the issue of future societies for years and completed fundamental research between 1998 and 2004. [8] It would not have been possible without testers and research subjects whose experience in technology and environments significantly contributed to the analysis and the ensuing development of new objects.

[8] sentha (*Seniorengerechte Technik im häuslichen Alltag* [Senior-friendly technology in the everyday household]), the DFG financed joint project run by the Berlin University of the Arts, the Berlin and Cottbus Technical University, and the Berlin Institute for Social Research, established parameters for future design—as a social project that would bring people and objects together.

Professor Ernst Pöppel, chair of the board of directors at the Institute for Medical Psychology in Munich, also maintains that we are getting older and more difficult to generalize. He also heads the Generation Research Project, GRP. Innovative technology should be developed in collaboration with industry, using multigenerational basic research. "It is essential to co-create with industry," says Pöppel. To provide a driving force for future projects, the generation researcher approaches everyday objects with completely new questions. He assumes the user perspective, rather than continuing to hope that people will simply just start using everything correctly, which is what industry still somehow believes. Pöppel believes that "it is important to develop people-friendly technology," which should adapt to the needs of (older) people, and not vice versa.

[9] http://www.seniorenfreundlich. de/seniorenprodukte.html *

The steadily increasing self-organization of users should not be underestimated. They often possess a sound education and lifelong experience. Glancing through the related forums and Internet portals reveals that experts from different generations offer assistance to and form networks with people of similar interests, because they want to continue being active in an ever-changing world. Otto Buchegger outlines an interesting formula on his website, "seniorenfreundlich" (senior-friendly) [9]: "size or typeface that is too small, colors that are too dark, too many symbols, too few (German language) texts, too many (often) unnecessary functions, plus expensive, difficult handling that requires too much strength, you have to bend down to operate something, you don't know what to do, the products make people look like idiots." Buchegger goes beyond criticizing and also gives advice: "Ease of learning is more important for seniors than ease of use. Of course, both are important goals, but if in doubt, it is better for the product to be easy to understand than fast to operate. If other compromises have to be made, then simply omit some functions. Just have as many as are necessary: as few as possible is a good motto here." Experts agree that having senior consultants as testers is essential for new product development.

Age as an Economic Factor or: Comfort for Everyone

It does not matter how you view it, the future looks old. And even if the limits of growth seem to have been reached, seniors form the renewable resource worldwide. "The fifty-plus population is the fastest growing segment worldwide. An aging society is the opportunity to invent the future of healthy, active living," [10] according to researchers at the AgeLab at MIT. Wherever you look: the USA, Europe, Asia, and in particular China with its courageous, yet soon to prove difficult, one-child policy, the classic age pyramid became a funnel long ago. Even highly developed social systems are not yet prepared for this transformation. Euphemisms, such as "pension shortfalls," conceal a drastic development. Old age poverty is again the order of the day. Already one third of all pensioners live below poverty level according to social researcher Professor Meinhard Miegel of the Bonn Institute for Economy and Society. [11] It is a frightening prognosis: in twenty-five years every second pensioner will receive an income of not more than the minimum level of unemployment benefit recommended by Germany's "Hartz IV" level (the German term for unemployment benefits). The lonely, poorly cared for, and dispossessed seniors are increasingly countered by active, even business-minded and high-earning seniors. "The two-class medical system is a reality today," writes ZDF German Television in a background report to its docu-soap *2030 — Aufstand der Alten* (2030 — revolt of the seniors) [12] on the gap between private and state patients. "There is a high probability that Germany will have to resort to rationing medical services in the future. In England, the National Health Services has already stopped covering certain operations for older people."

10   http://web.mit.edu/agelab/about_agelab.shtml

11—12   http://www.zdf.de/ZDFde/inhalt/8/0,1872,4295080,00.html

Looking at figures, which can be interpreted very differently according to standpoint and interest: in Germany for example, 144,000 more people died in 2006 than were born. By 2030, the population will have decreased from circa 82.5 million to 78 million. Absolute numbers say little about the changes occurring within a society, after the number of over 65-year-olds rises to fifty percent, from approximately 16 million today to 24 million. Life expectancy in 2030 will be eighty-one years of age for men and eighty-six for women. Older, wiser, and more discerning, or merely senile and fragile? The coming years will show. Ending up in a nursing home is one of the most horrifying thoughts today besides unemployment or disability. The Deutsche Institut für Menschenrechte (DIMR) (German Institute for Human Rights) denounces the devastating conditions in nursing homes. "Almost one half of the 600,000 residents in nursing homes are undernourished and do not receive enough fluids." [13]

13 http://www.zdf.de/ZDFde/inhalt/8/0,1872,4295080,00.html

There is a turnabout coming, however, summarized in AgeLab's powerful motto, "Aging: A Global Opportunity to Live Better," which for many is little more than an American invocation to optimism. A call for quality, for the good life, which today is increasingly difficult to achieve in a society based on growth and acceleration, on the fundamental values of youth, and which prescribes these for age as well.

Will standards shift? The idea that everything young and beautiful must also be good has prevailed for a long time. But how will this function in the future? The attractiveness of younger people will persist, precisely because there will be fewer of them. In fact, their value will most likely increase. On the other hand, the majority will no longer be able to dictate body awareness and values to older people. Because ultimately the latter have the money. And the time. And the ideas. Some companies have already recognized this fact and have positioned themselves for the fifty-plus market. "Because beauty has no age limit," a claim made by Dove's commercials for their "pro age" beauty product line. The company substantiates this with findings from a June 2006 study, in which 1,450 women between the ages of fifty and sixty-four were interviewed on the subject of beauty and aging. Eighty-seven percent of all those over fifty felt "too young to be marked as 'old'." This was followed by the decisive postscript: "They would welcome society changing its view about women and aging."

Dove pro age
Advertising Campaign for
Beauty Products

The very successful and pleasant Dove
advertising campaign shows us how
conditioned our perception actually is.
Naked older women are suddenly
the talk of the town. Obviously a break
in taboo for our youth- and fitness-
obsessed society. Age is beautiful.

Gold Rush Mood in the Japanese Silver Market

The economic system is rethinking and has recognized age as both an opportunity and a growth market. The so-called silver market is at the fore with regard to household income and investment. The market report entitled *Senior Finance*, published by the Cologne-based consultants BBE on July 14, 2006, concludes that the over fifty-five generation comprise "about half of all private assets." They command "over four-tenths of private household income. Two-thirds own real estate, seventy-five percent of which is completely paid off." [14] The prognoses: the number of seniors is increasing along with their financial power. Their wealth will have increased by approximately twenty-eight percent to 2.9 billion euros, just between 2006 and 2011. Meaning that the "percentage of wealth in private financial assets belonging to those over fifty-five will increase to fifty-five percent." Little of this ends up in piggy banks or is stuffed under the mattress. Expenditure is part and parcel of this growing target group with its rapidly expanding demands. The hedonistic lifestyle of a generation that does not see itself as old-timers clashes with a lack of social acceptance, a lack of product selection, and an equally growing group of dispossessed and impoverished citizens. Moreover, the oft-cited consumer abstinence is — purely statistically speaking — untrue. Quite the contrary: the "old" will spend and already do. Sixty-five- to Seventy-five-year-olds spend eighty-four percent of their available income on consumer goods: "fifty percent of all German new cars are purchased by people who are fifty or older, and this rises to eighty percent of the buyers of luxury class cars." [15]

14 *Senior Finance. BBE-Branchenreport*. Cologne, 2006.

15 Scheytt, Stefan: "Woopies. Sie haben Geld. Sie haben Zeit. Und alte Menschen können noch eine Menge brauchen." *brand eins* 9/2005. *

There is no other group more "heterogenous than the senior group," according to the Berlin-based sociologist Hartmut Häußermann. [16] Their lifestyle and shopping habits are similarly differentiated. There is no other target group quite so discerning, well funded, and above all so divergent as the so-called seniors. And none so well off and ready to spend money. Today, according to minister Ursula von der Leyen, the money spent by the over-sixty generation comprises one third of all private expenditure. "By the year 2050, their share of private expenditure, based purely on demography, will have risen to as much as forty percent." [17] Von der Leyen concludes with a call for action: "Whoever understands this challenge as a great opportunity and develops something new will have the possibility of profiting from a global market."

Europe and the USA are nowhere near the top of this field. Japan is the leading nation in the elderly market. With the world's highest life expectancy plus a very low birth rate, the Land of the Rising Sun has long been influenced by two expressions: *shirubâ sangyô*, "silver industry," and *shirubâ maketto*, "silver market." Rethinking began here very early. Toward the end of the 1970s at the latest, "public awareness about the problem of a rapidly aging population was very high," according to a study by the German Ministry for Family, Seniors, Women and Youth. [18] Here, earlier than in other countries, companies recognized the significance of the market and its specific demands, particularly regarding the medical and health care industry. There are, however, potential areas of growth, other than those core health care sectors, rooted in gerontology and medical care. They mushroomed after the all-powerful economic ministry, METI (Ministry for Economy, Trade and Industry), recognized the senior economy as a growth market and made it official by "transforming population aging into a growth machine (*seichô enjin*)." [19] From Panasonic to the cosmetic giant Shiseido, seniors are viewed as customers to be won by means of product innovation and aggressive product advertising. This is rooted in a fundamental awareness that has a head start on most western societies. Japan tackles the challenge of aging so that the amenities of a low-barrier or even barrier-free environment, as well as new, intuitively operated, simple appliances are a benefit to all. The unfortunate but resonant prejudice we harbor toward senior-friendly, or in other words "senile" products is nonexistent in Japan. This head start in development is both very real and tangible. For a good ten years, Japan has been producing so-called *Kyôyo hin* products, or "universally usable" goods that fulfill all the requirements of

16 Häußermann, Hartmut: "Altern in der Stadt" (Aging in the city). In: *Wohnen im Alter. Visionen, Realitäten, Erfahrungen* (Senior living. Visions, reality, experience). Oberste Baubehörde im Bayerischen Staatsministerium des Inneren (Supreme building authority of the Bavarian State Ministry of the Interior) (ed.): Documentation of the seminar on February 21, 2006, pp. 21—40; here p. 22. *

17 Schmidt-Ruhland, Karin (ed.): *Pack ein — pack aus — pack zu. Neue Verpackungen für Alt und Jung* (Pack in — pack out — take hold. New packaging for the young and old). Berlin University of the Arts, 2006, p. 10. *

18 Gerling, Vera; Conrad, Harald: *Wirtschaftskraft Alter in Japan. Handlungsfelder und Strategien* (The economic power of the elderly in Japan. Fields of action and strategies). Study commissioned by the Bundesministerium für Familie, Senioren, Frauen und Jugend, 2002, p. 6. *

19 *Wirtschaftskraft Alter in Japan*, p. 18. *

Universal Design and thus pervade and alter everyday life as a whole.

This is based on the philosophy that no one should be left behind and that progress in user-friendliness should not be seen as catering to the old or disabled, but rather as an enhancement of the quality of life for the population as a whole. Since 1999, the Kyôyo-hin Foundation has overseen a growing market; its guidelines were very influential for the publication in 2001 of **ISO-Norm 71** — "Guidelines for standards developers to address the needs of older persons and persons with disabilities." [20] Statistics verify the success of *Kyôyo-hin* products, which, compared to other standard care products, more than doubled their volume in Japan between 1996 and 2000. [21]

The **ADF** (Accessibility Design Foundation) points out that in today's day and age design comprises more than aesthetics. It is a matter of fundamental magnitude, of access to society and its communicative environments; accessible products and services have become key terms in the industry. [22]

It is no wonder that Japan has an organization called **ESPA** (Elderly Service Providers Association) which labels different product types that — according to definition — either comprise products and services exclusively for older people or those that cover "the needs of healthy, active seniors as well as those of seniors in need of care." [23]

20 www.iso.org

21 *Wirtschaftskraft Alter in Japan*, p. 13.

22 "With the advent of an unprecedented aging society, the needs for AD products and services have been intensified. At the same time, the word 'accessible products/services' has come to be regarded as a key term for the industries." Kyôyo-Hin Foundation, Japan. PDF at: http://www.kyoyohin. org/09_foreign/English_ver.pdf

23 *Wirtschaftskraft Alter in Japan*, p. 12.*

24 *Wirtschaftskraft Alter in Japan*, p. 22.*

These should soon play as insignificant a role as special applications, for instance a nurse robot, or a navigation system for wheel chairs developed by Kusada International, a Tokyo-based company. This is a market that is difficult to understand and serve since the "needs of Japanese older people are too complex and heterogeneous for economic mass production," as stated by the organizers of a study on the Far East silver market. [24] Developing *Kyôyo-hin* products is more crucial than perfecting rehabilitation engineering, it places user-friendliness for all population groups at the core.

The Fluke: the Porsche Cayenne — Comfort for All

The so-called "senior" Porsche, Cayenne, is the proof. Products will not sell because they have been designed for older people, they will sell nonetheless. An elevated boarding height, back-friendly seats, and good overview are all by-products of a luxury sports utility vehicle for the discerning customer. No one ever considered an aggressive campaign to advertise the vehicle as senior-friendly. And for good reason. The Cayenne shows how much the industry can profit from mature target groups — and from users as a whole. Instead of trimming down products to fit ever-smaller markets and including the very last splinter group, an unintentionally broad approach shows how a company can forge a relationship with customers. Forget rehabilitation engineering. Forget excluding and stigmatizing customers. Long live comfort for all. It is not the first time that a particularly comfortable new product succeeds. What at first seems like purely special solutions end up being universal. One example here is the low-floor technology used in public transportation that has become common in buses and trams. What was once developed as a standard only for people with limited mobility is now a popular convenience for everyone. They also help reduce the average time needed to board the bus or tram, which, in turn, is an additional benefit for the bus company.

Yet we continue to walk into an aesthetic trap: the idea that small is beautiful has not yet exhausted itself, but it has lost its significance. Youth is still considered the market-dominating target group. Particularly in the western hemisphere, attractiveness is immediately connected with freshness, youth, and activity. It is no wonder that even older young-at-hearts do not want to forgo anything associated with this image of youth; indeed, according to conservative predictions, in 2020 one third of all motorists and cyclists will be over sixty. There is now suddenly a fourth period of life after childhood, the intern generation, the career life, followed by retirement by seventy. It is only then that our intellectual and physical resources begin to diminish. Fragile seniors, however, are convinced that age is a negative thing. Any object focusing on deficits will find itself in a dangerous downward spiral. Rehabilitation engineering and alleged senior-friendly products will disappear in the future, while today's perception of age makes way for a much more discriminating view. No one becomes old overnight; we grow old gradually. For many years we compensate for the permanent changes in our bodies and intellects until we reach and cross certain thresholds. Until this happens, it is questionable whether we actually need senior-friendly products if designers are following the principles of Universal Design from the onset.

Scandinavia has long been a forerunner of social change that is reflected in everyday objects and environments. If an ergonomic bread knife can be found at IKEA, then it is obvious why there is no need for specifically senior-friendly products. An ergonomic tool suddenly signalizes a cultural shift that does not focus on rehabilitation supplies and, purely as a sideline, replaces stigma with broad access. Health-oriented advertisements are already making an effort to modernize the image of older people. There is a great need for new products, as well as the related services and consultation. Age is now an opportunity, not a burden, for an economic system that increasingly wants to retain its employees' experience-based expertise, rather than sacrifice it when those workers turn fifty. Designers and sociologists agree that tomorrow's older people are different to those of the past. Economists maintain that something else is needed to create a market: self-sufficiency. New possibilities open up as soon as patients become active consumers and paying users. People who pay for their needs out of their own pockets are more critical and discerning than a patient who is allotted something, and hence is unaware of its value (price).

The new world begins with comfort-oriented objects that will trigger greater changes. Yet we still have to question everything from the ticket machine to the cooking pot, from a user interface to an ironing board. This will benefit all users. Manufacturers afraid of age are afraid of their own shadow. They have to tackle the issue more aggressively. And those who laugh off universal products, as niche products with a guaranteed negative image that will not sell, will fall behind. Older people are anything but guinea pigs; they are mature consumers and, as such, are seismographs for bad design. In short they are the ideal partners in the effort to optimize products for the benefit of all.

Mathias Knigge, partner in the Hamburg agency grauwert
on promoting and developing products for the elderly

OH   **How long have you been working in the area of Universal Design?**

MK   For almost ten years. I started as a research associate on the "sentha" research project at the University of the Arts in Berlin. At that time, we were researching the subject of household products for the elderly. Our brief was to create prototypes that would not conspicuously seem like products for "old people," but that would serve as examples to show how a senior-friendly future world might look like.

OH   **What was the key to this?**

MK   Acceptance. It is vital for anything involving Universal Design. You have to go beyond pure barrier-free buildings or attempting to relieve older people's deficits. It is really about creating additional uses and a suitable design. In this regard, understanding age-specific changes forms the basis of our knowledge. Simultaneously, we worked on methods that would actively include older people in the development of products.

OH   **By using surveys?**

MK   We weren't interested in quantitative questionnaires. We wanted to get closer to the source, and therefore we examined the world of the elderly at home. Where were the problem areas, what needed to be changed? Where can prototypes or products be introduced to be of assistance and then be evaluated?

OH   **Ten years sounds like a long time. What did you achieve during this period?**

MK   We experienced the beginnings. Back then it was a purely experimental academic project that was hardly noticed by the public.

Age was not yet an issue. It was just starting to penetrate public awareness as the research project was coming to an end in 2003. Initially, it was approached very generally in talk shows and in books that dealt with the generation issue, then it was eventually studied more in detail and issues were being examined such as which products are appropriate for a population that is growing older.

OH **Looking at products now, what has actually changed? Have there been any milestones?**

MK It is a rather gradual process of many small steps. Everyone is working on it, but few do so openly. Coming on the market with products explicitly for the elderly is still to be avoided at all costs. That's why many changes can only be recognized with an educated eye.

OH **Why do so few companies advertise senior-friendly design? Are they afraid of their products being stigmatized?**

MK A core issue today is how to discreetly communicate good solutions that will make life easier for elderly people. Older people don't feel comfortable talking openly about their possible deficits, yet it's still necessary to communicate the functions of a product to its potential buyers.

So that Design Succeeds

OH **Can you name some examples of successful design?**

MK One example is the ALNO kitchen company with their "My Way" product line. Three or four years ago, the first workshops were held in companies and then a competition. Now the kitchen is available in stores. The improvements are in the details: an additional handle, a cutting board that can be raised ten centimeters. Also good shelves, pull-out drawers for crates of water, or a higher dishwashing machine. The communication is correct: not for the elderly, but for individualists.

OH   **Hence the equation, "not for the old, but for everyone"?**

MK   Older people will see it as a significant improvement; younger people will think it's simply more comfortable. This allows us to communicate "comfort and ease" and categorize all special solutions under the term "barrier-free." Such products are not very popular among the masses anyway, because they are only available in small series and often look rather different.

OH   **Do all-purpose solutions set universality against comfort?**

MK   The idea of additional value is important. This is something that one's own brand does not destroy, and it's more appealing to consumers if they do not have to buy a specifically senior-friendly product line. Psychology plays a role here, because no one likes to admit having a shortcoming. As a rule, a person decides on certain products at a time when age is not yet an issue. Shortly before entering a nursing home, when the apartment no longer functions, a new kitchen will not help you remain in your own apartment for another ten years. But at fifty-five or sixty it is possible and necessary to determine the problem points and begin preparing the apartment. The advantages will be beneficial well into old age.

Japan is More Advanced

OH   **How does Europe compare with Japan?**

MK   Japan is more advanced in this area, and they manufacture more products that follow Universal Design principles. The Japanese recognized the age issue much earlier. A consortium of leading companies founded an association for Universal Design to undertake joint research activities. However, there is a massive cultural difference that makes it difficult.

OH   **What do the Japanese want and what do the Europeans want?**

MK   Technology is viewed very differently in Japan, and its supportive potential is more highly valued. Here, a toilet that also measures the blood sugar count would be like George Orwell's 1984 or considered constant surveillance. Likewise, a teapot that sends a text message to relatives when tea is not regularly made, or, in other words, when a person is not drinking regularly, would be regarded as interfering. Or robots that look like cuddly toys. I don't know if this is better or worse, because a world such as this can also confound me sometimes. Many things cannot be directly conveyed, but they are economically successful, for one because they had an earlier start. Toshiba produced an easy-to-load washing machine with a drum that is tilted at fifteen degrees. It's a small but important detail. The drum's opening is also twenty percent larger and the symbols are bigger. Japan is opening a different world, yet if you compare different products, the more playful ones can also be strange and confusing.

OH **Let's talk numbers. How large is the market for Universal Design?**

MK At the moment there are more than twenty million people over the age of sixty in Germany. And in 2030, it is predicted that this group will represent one third of the population. On the other hand, the population as a whole is shrinking, meaning there will be fewer young consumers. The financial resources of the over fifty-five-year-old group are also very good. According to one study, they have access to more than 2.3 billion euros in financial assets. But ultimately figures are not what truly count, because Universal Design does not aim to sell only to the older generation. It's about the product being interesting for everyone, including the old.

OH **Advances are being made in the telecommunications market. But how useful are XXL size mobile phones such as "Katharina das Große" (Catherine the Great)?**

MK That is a gray area. The user interface is clearly made for older people, but according to Universal Design criteria it is ten percent too large. It communicates that the product is unique because it does not comply with the aesthetics of a real product series. The emphasis on very large buttons suddenly alludes to a shortcoming. It wouldn't appeal to a forty-year-old and, hence, misses an opportunity. A design that includes others and their needs would be effective in this case.

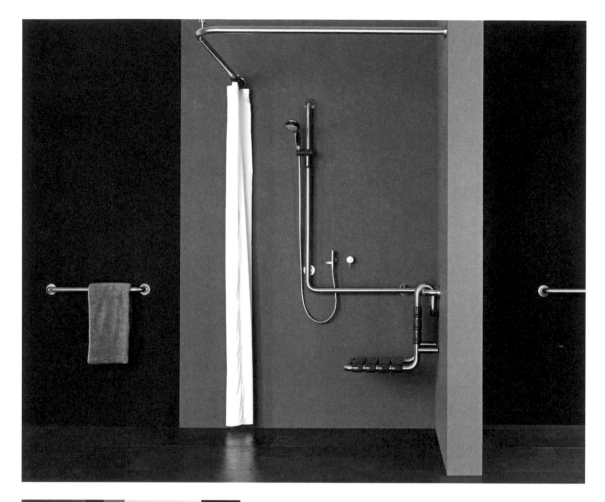

Range 805
Barrier-free Bathroom by HEWI

On-grade access without difficult
doorsills, handles, and optional assisted
seating. That is the standard bathroom of
the future, which also does not exclude
any aesthetic considerations. Clear forms
and easy-to-clean fixtures make the
bathroom pleasant to the eye and hand.

OH   **Why are no mass producers getting involved in Universal Design?**

MK   For one, because the ringtone business for people under twenty-three is so massive that they can afford to ignore other fields. On the other hand, consumers still seem happy to purchase products that will be of little use later. The revolution hasn't happened. The first company to design a mobile telephone that is easy to use and beautifully designed will be the winner, if they can reach both the middle- aged and elderly target groups via communication and sales.

OH   **So the big guys are waiting?**

MK   They may even wait until the problem is almost solved. There is still a lot in the pipeline, but they are waiting for small providers to make all the initial mistakes and create a market. They'll be able to enter that market later with ease, after older people have taken over the mobile phone market from the younger ones. The issue is this: until now, user-friendliness has been sacrificed to functional diversity. But in the long run, it will be impossible to get around Universal Design products. The area of kitchen and bath fixtures is a forerunner. Here, the focus has already completely shifted from handicapped accessible to barrier-free, and now to comfort bath facilities. User-friendliness and good design make the idea very appealing.

OH   **From the bathroom to the apartment to the wide, wide world?**

MK   We are hopeful. There is certainly enough determination.

UNIVERSAL DESIGN IN PRACTICE:
GEARED TO AGE FROM HEAD TO FOOT

<u>Seventy Overnight: Shopping in an Age Simulation Suit</u>

15.40 p.m.   Ready. Should I take off my pants? "No, you don't have to, but please have a seat." Dr. Roland Schoeffel spreads a shiny pair of silver overalls on the floor. It could be an astronaut suit, an early one, like the one John Glenn wore when he circled the earth. I slide one leg into the suit carefully. Then the other leg. He fastens the Velcro bands as soon as I'm inside the oversize suit. Now it's fairly tight. There are plates on my joints. It's harder to bend my arms and legs. Now come the weights. Schoeffel grins and slides iron rods into pockets in the arms, legs, and chest. They look like chocolate bars. Each weighs 100 grams, making a total of fifteen kilos of iron. Fifteen years older. Immovable. "How does it feel suddenly to have less strength?" Strange.

15.51 p.m.   Now the gloves, then the glasses over my head, and the earphones. Then comes the collar. I now know why older people have a harder time moving and turning their heads. Schoeffel's voice reaches me as though through cotton wool. The office seems to have shrunk. "How does it feel?" asks the developer. I stand up. Carefully. Step by step. Like honey, as if you are walking through a viscous mass. I feel claustrophobic. Is this it? A prisoner in your own body. Houston, I have a problem.

15.55 p.m.   Stay calm. Just walk down the stairs. Step by step. "Hold on," someone murmurs behind me. Someone is pulling on my feet, some-one doesn't want me to lift my hand. I push on. Now go into the cellar. Get a case of beer. Alcohol-free. Where is the light switch? The empty cases have to go in the car. Now to the beverage store. Bend down and pull out the cases from under the shelf. Ok. Now in the car.

16.03 p.m.   I have to be careful not to trip over things. The suit has slipped over my shoes. How do I open the trunk? A tiny button. Watch out for the hatchback, then put the beer inside. Now get in, into the back. There is no door back here. Everything seems so foreign, so diffuse. I would not be able to drive like this. I'm glad when I finally sit down.

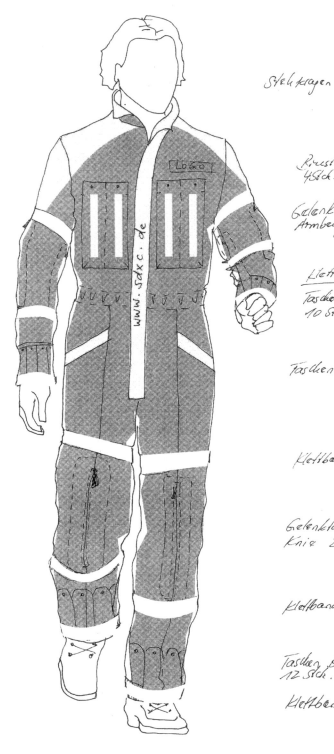

Age Simulation Suit
Designed by SD&C GmbH

Weights on arms and legs, tinted yellow eyeglasses, and earplugs help create the sensation of diminishing strength and sensory abilities.

Stehkragen

Brusttasche Bleigewichte
4 Stck.

Gelenktasche
Armbeuge/Ellenbogen

Klettband

Taschen Bleigewichte
10 Stck.

Tascheneingriff

Klettband

Gelenktasche
Knie 25 x 4 cm

Klettband

Taschen Bleigewichte
12 Stck.

Klettband

16.09 p.m.   In front of the beverage store. Panic. I can't get out. Something is holding me down. Of course, undo the belt. Swing a leg around the front seat, climb out of the car, and trudge toward the entrance with the beer in hand. "Look for a new case," commands Roland Schoeffel. Easier said than done. Everything looks the same. There are towers of beverage piled high and the signs are blurred. I can barely recognize anything. Will it really feel like this later? Cola, cases of water, beer. Where is the alcohol-free beer? I bend down with difficulty and start again from the beginning.

16.14 p.m.   Roland Schoeffel takes my hand. "It's over there." Thank you. I bend down again; the full case is a challenge. It weighs a ton. Now I have to pay. €11.95. Schoeffel gives me the wallet. Find 50 euros. I want to ask if they have change. But I'm too ambitious. I look for a coin. Is this two euros? Questioningly, I show it to the sales person. I was lucky.

What is the suit supposed to do? "It was developed to give one a vague idea of how it feels to be old," answers Schoeffel. In order to gather scientific data, it has to be adapted to fit the wearer exactly. Even then it can only give a partial idea of the future world, after the whites of your eyes have turned yellow, your hearing has faded, muscle mass has shrunk, your sense of touch has diminished, and every step you take is an effort. Tomorrow's objects and environments have to be able to adapt after your strength, mobility, and senses have diminished.

Despite research and Universal Design principles, 100 percent user-friendliness is not always possible. Ergonomic experts agree that there will always be a sharp edge somewhere. After working on a machine for a long time, Schoeffel and his team managed ninety-five percent. "We removed some buttons and it still works fine." The 55-year-old studied psychology, computer science, and anthropology and was head of the Ergonomics and User Interface Design department at Siemens before becoming self-employed in 2002 and setting up his company, SD&C GmbH. There is a bowl of fruit jelly gums behind the notebook. Red, green, yellow. "I need them sometimes," says Roland Schoeffel and pops one in his mouth. This is exactly how the suit feels, as if you are packed in jelly.

Shopping in an age simulation suit:
the author as guinea pig.

Bosch-Siemens household appliances rarely advertised products that had been worked on by engineers, designers, and psychologists. In the mid 1990s, that meant comfort, explains Schoeffel, and the catalog showed senior models standing next to the dishwasher with the easy-to-load tabs box. That was it. No Universal Design label, no special name for senior-friendly functions. Back then they began their own version of an age simulation suit, using ski goggles, gloves, and protective ear-flaps, which made subjects immediately thirty years older. The suit was designed to enable its wearers to experience the world after their maximum performance had peaked. Managers were particularly impressed, says Schoeffel, when they "were able to feel first-hand what it was like to be old." Schoeffel remembers how a colleague had to unload the dishwasher in a bending position and fell over onto his back like a beetle bug. "We need to change something." A realization based on one's own experience — and we seem to find it difficult to put ourselves in someone else's shoes, especially if these are linked in any way to limitations, handicaps, and suffering and are in conflict with one's own thinking and feelings. What can designers and the industry learn from this research? It is a matter of a new perception and a willingness to leave the beaten path. Large buttons, trimmed down functions, and oversized appliances are not enough if they are not sexy. Aesthetics has nothing to do with age, and design is meant to help products stand out on the market, not to ostracize. Universal Design will define a new balance between form and ergonomics by never separating the two, and allowing both to enhance one another. In the future, superficial styling will have a rough time of it, as will marketing-driven, hypothetical product innovations that, in fact, are little more than technical gadgets.

An Eye for an Eye, an Ear for an Ear

It is a matter of the whole. Eye, ear, hand, foot have to work in unison if we wish to be a part of this increasingly complex world. There is however a pragmatic reason for the following chapter perhaps sounding contrary to this hypothesis, or even seeming like a quasi-atomistic fragmentation of people's senses and limbs. Yet, if the point is to evaluate individual innovations and create a basis for comparing those we encounter in the future, then categories do offer invaluable advantages — not least because this is where architecture, interior architecture, and design interact and therefore pursue a unity on another, higher level. Design offers the unity; its goals are humanist. It should no longer be regarded as a mere aesthetic shell or a compensational factor for a heartless society that replaces togetherness with technology. It forms part of a change. It is a catalyst and a product of the new. Design is nothing more than one part of an ongoing process.

25—28 Burckhardt, Lucius: "Design ist unsichtbar." In: *Design ist unsichtbar*. Edited by Helmut Gsöllpointer, Angela Hareiter, and Laurids Ortner. Österreichisches Institut für Visuelle Gestaltung (Austrian Institute for Visual Design). Vienna, Löcker, 1981, pp. 13—20; here p. 18. *

Not everything will be simply assigned to a category, and some readers may feel that another, definitive aspect is missing: the human intellect. Yet it shines out of the numerous innovations by designers, who have focused their efforts so intensely on developing future substructures that they did not stop at products, but instead dedicated themselves to analyzing and advancing social systems — as if influenced by Lucius Burckhardt's criticism of the Ulm Academy of Design, or better still had implemented it. "The Ulm solutions," wrote Burckhardt in 1981 in his famous essay "Design ist unsichtbar" (Design is invisible), "were technocratic. They were based on a radical analysis of the purpose to be fulfilled, yet did not place the purpose in a higher context." [25] Burckhardt presented unsuccessful design approaches that focused on the object without considering the whole or, as he put it, "divided the world into objects rather than problems." [26] Hence, Burckhardt even thought that "evil objects" existed, disintegrating objects, such as cars, which "make us dependent upon systems that ultimately plunder or abandon us." [27] The following examples are precisely the opposite of this approach. The objects and environments presented here endeavor to ensure that everyone participates in society, even if he or she ultimately does not meet one of Burckhardt's requirements. Half jokingly, he enlists a small intellectual experiment. Why work at designing modern forks if it is actually a matter of living together, and why not design kitchens "that inspire the guest to help the host chop onions." [28]

Why not? Perhaps the many detailed solutions are merely small steps toward a Universal Design that is all encompassing and ubiquitous, a true mirror of our society? Objects will be equipped with intelligence and networked. Tomorrow's world is a smart world.

Smart Home — Intelligence in Objects

For sometime now, smart home has been the magic term for developers who dream of building intelligent homes that serve and devotedly supervise their occupants. A clever system is responsible for security and safety. If the occupant falls, for instance, and cannot call for help, it sends an automatic emergency call. Whether it suits us or not, tomorrow's world will be significantly different from today's. However, we will continue to adapt and develop core elements from today's day and age. Communication is the key to the future. It will be all-encompassing and ubiquitous. In addition to human dialog, machine communication will emerge that will depend on the widespread, rudimentary intelligence of objects. At the heart of this new world of communication, decentralized radio chips will transmit information about their wearers: location, content, or weight. But there are divided opinions about **Radio Frequency Identification** (RFID) technology. On the one hand, critics fear that radio chips will become the most subtle and all-encompassing consumer surveillance system since the invention of the written word. Data protection agencies are also skeptical about the corporate information-gathering mania, which, for the first time in history, can recognize the shopping patterns of individuals. Yet on the other hand, many already acknowledge the great progress made in the automatic identification of objects and living organisms via applied or implanted transponders. But let us assume that the chips are in fact helpful to people and, together with bar code scanners, can replace illegible medical packaging labels and display relevant content on a screen, provide dose information, make key rings obsolete, or — in an extreme case — even save the lives of people who, for instance, got lost walking through the woods? RFID is more than the mere automatic collection of data, yet the first steps are indeed going in that direction. It is also not yet sure whether the line between security and surveillance will be crossed after all. However, one thing is certain: tomorrow's world will replace hardware with software. ID and keys can be replaced by biometric and RFID-Based Access Control Systems. The American Food and Drug Administration are planning to equip medication with radio labels to protect them against counterfeits, as Karin Pollack reported in 2005 in *brand eins*. Intel, however, tested the RFID chip for "its capability as an ubiquitous attendant — even at home." [29]

Years ago, the radio alarm clock was a primitive, one-sided form of communication that gave us a preliminary taste of what lay ahead. The good essence inherent in all objects is tangible here. Felix Wiesner, a 24-year-old designer from Trier, was awarded second place in the first nationwide competition, "Pack ein — pack aus — pack zu. Neue Verpackungen für Alt und Jung" (Pack in — pack out — take hold. New packaging for the old and young) [30] for his Wassergeist. The idea behind the **Memowasserflasche Wassergeist** (Memo water bottle Water Spirit), with its textured surface for easy handling, its easy-to-open-and-close cap, and candy-colored coding representing the content of the bottles, is do not forget to drink. A corresponding bracelet with a vibrating alarm regularly reminds the wearer to drink fluids. Wiesner's reminder system does not only assist the elderly, but it does target this group. Moreover, it is tangible and hence conventional compared to the networked intelligence systems of the brave new world.

Recruiting unusually intelligent objects as helping hands and invisible guardian angels also indicates a new path for design. The first signs of this — studies and prototypes — can be traced as far back as 2002 when communication providers and designers were researching new methods of personally storing and holding data. [31] David Tonge, then associate partner at Pentagram Design, developed a design study for AT&T, the American telecommunications giant. The brief was to study how the flow of information influences our everyday lives. Kylie, Joe, Phyllis, and Lars are the names of the human models who shed light on their preferred, representative key areas of school (knowledge), health, leisure, and retail trade. Pensioner Joe wears a sphygmomanometer on his T-shirt; his

29 Pollack, Karin: "Was ist eigentlich RFID?" (What is RFID really?) *brand eins* 1/2005. *

30 Schmidt-Ruhland, Karin (ed.): *Pack ein — pack aus — pack zu. Neue Verpackungen für Alt und Jung*. Berlin University of the Arts, 2006.

31 Herwig, Oliver: "Adressen und andere Kleinigkeiten." (Addresses and other insignificants things). *Designreport* 5/02.

Memo Water Bottle
Water Spirit
Water Bottle designed by
Felix Wiesner

A vibrating armband regularly
reminds the wearer to drink. It
won second prize in the 2006
competition "Pack ein — pack aus
— pack zu. Neue Verpackungen
für Alt und Jung."

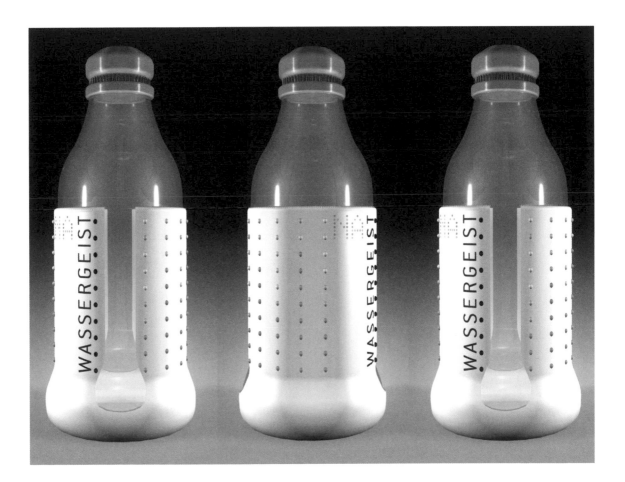

cutlery counts his caloric intake and records what he eats. Phyllis, a mother of three, wears a so-called **Personal shopper** on her shoulder bag that knows her profile, her day's appointment schedule, and can also communicate with shelves in stores. It reminds her about "the things she forgot to get," as it claims in the accompanying text, or advises her about "what she might need" for the evening's party, or simply on everything that she would "normally buy."

A brave, beautiful new world. What we do with it is our choice, but first the ubiquitous intelligence in objects will make life easier. And that is not necessarily a bad thing, regardless of age.

Personal Shopper
Design Study by David Tonge

The designer presented his Personal Shopper in 2002. It stores individual user and shopper profiles and communicates these to the product world via Radio Frequency Identification (RFID). The question here, is how can we interact with our environment and how can we organize our future life?

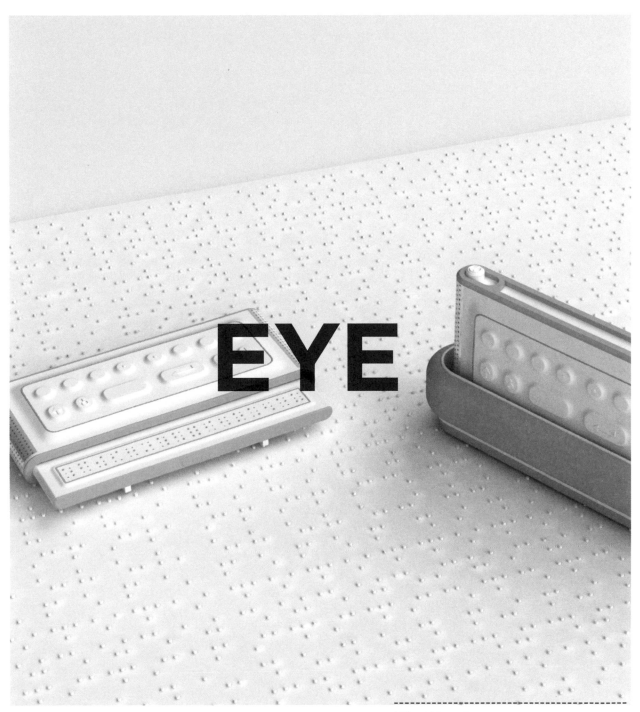

EYE

Blind Touch
Direct-translation Reading Machine
designed by Chun-Chiang Huang

Voice and other sounds can be recorded by
a mere push of the button. The device trans-
lates the spoken word into Braille that is
printed out as ticker tape on the underside.

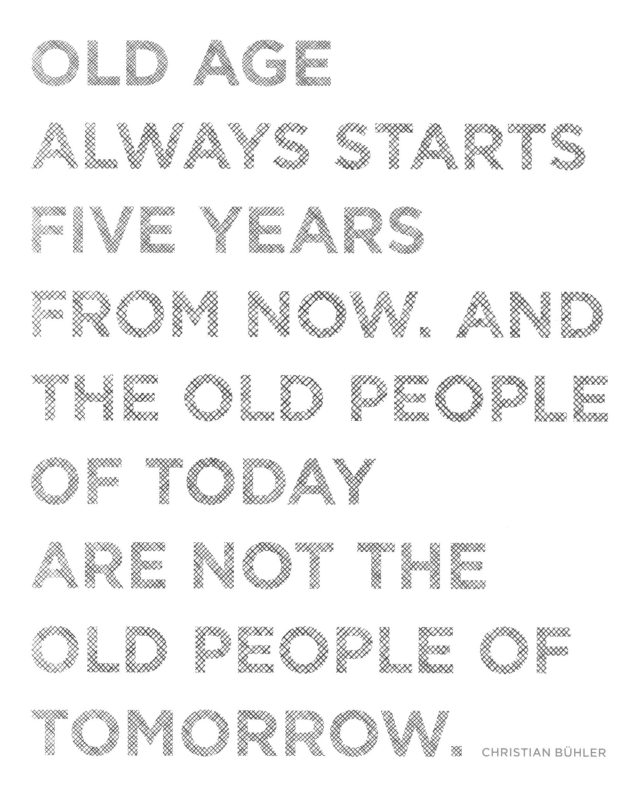

OLD AGE ALWAYS STARTS FIVE YEARS FROM NOW. AND THE OLD PEOPLE OF TODAY ARE NOT THE OLD PEOPLE OF TOMORROW. CHRISTIAN BÜHLER

Eye

The world is flat and, since the computer began to govern ever more areas of life, has often been packed into a nineteen or twenty-one inch frame. Its user interfaces and program versions define the limits of our perception. For a long time users have been satisfied by standard solutions that they either adapted with more or less effort to fit their needs or simply had to accept. The much-praised intelligence of products remained obsolete and intuitive, self-explanatory surfaces and programs were the exception. [32] Using a computer still means learning to deal with the computer, and even open-source projects such as Linux have yet to change this.

32 Even after usability had been introduced to the product world and adopted by different companies. Microsoft Corporation had one of the largest Accessibility work groups worldwide and was therefore awarded an important distinction in 2000: "The accessibility group within Microsoft has grown to be the largest group of its size in any company in the world. This group has made Windows 2.0 accessible for people with impaired hearing and dexterity; it has created an Access Pack for Microsoft Windows, an add-on package that includes features to enhance operating the keyboard and the mouse; improved Access Facilities for Windows 3.0 and 3.1; added closed captioning and audio description technology to make all of its multimedia products accessible to the deaf, hard of hearing and blind users." http://www.disabilityworld.org/June-July2000/access/Awards.html

33 The Fraunhofer Institute for Applied Information Technology gives tips about the relevant norms and includes information presentation, user interfaces, dialog control by means of menus and direct manipulation. http://www.fit-fuer-usability.de/tipps/software/information/02.html

Usability and computers are two worlds that still have to be united. Norms however do exist for designing software (ISO 9241 parts 12 to 17) and the recommendations derived from this, [33] as well as for guidelines for (senior-friendly) digital information design. The National Institute on Aging (NIA) and the National Library of Medicine is responsible for a particularly influential example. [34] However, some experts are concerned about design paternalism and increased restrictions on design freedom, which would ultimately lead to sacrificing aesthetics. Marc Hümmer, editor and founder of the online initiative "Fit for Usability" of the Fraunhofer Institute for Applied Information Technology, [35] argues that besides functional usability, hedonistic aspects such as pleasure and motivation also play an important role. In the first usability tests, participants felt "patronized by such design." His mandate: computer users should under no circumstances be labeled "old." "Design solutions must consider this aspect." [36]

34 Recommendations for designing senior-friendly websites: www.nlm.nih.gov/pubs/checklist.pdf

35 "Fit für Usability" is the online initiative of the Fraunhofer Institute for Applied Information Technology: http://www.fit-fuer-usability.de

36 Discussion with Marc Hümmer.

37 Mitchell, William J.: *City of Bits. Space, Place and the Infobahn*. MIT Press, Cambridge, MA, 1996.

How are interactive systems or special interfaces developing? Back in the autumn of 1969, a young academic assistant at UCLA was working next to a mainframe computer at the end of a corridor that was implanted with a small IMP (Interface Messaging Processor) — this was the first node for ARPAnet (Advanced Research Projects Agency Network). The student's name was William J. Mitchell. Soon after he became professor of architecture and media sciences. Mitchell later described the big bang of today's modern digital universe, as the grandfather of the modern Internet began his work. His classic book, *City of Bits*, [37] draws the conclusions. It does not merely convey simple ideas of urban planning and architecture to the developing digital world, but rather justifies our sensorium for the possibilities and limits of the networked world as a whole. Much has happened since 1995 when the book was first published. But Mitchell's prognosis still remains true. Citizens have become Internet users, who organize themselves into web communities such as MySpace — a network of over sixty million surfers, social groups, and friends. The city as a metaphor for community has been salvaged on the Internet with Second Life. Here, 3D becomes 2D — a flat world with access to the last hidden corners of the human psyche, and we still operate it using the computer industry's most standard tools: the keyboard and mouse. [38]

38 Bill Moggridge's standard work describes the history, development, and possibilities of input devices and user interfaces: *Designing Interactions*. MIT Press, Cambridge, MA, 2007.

Its success story has obviously not yet come to an end, but the computer industry is already experimenting with new (input) media and interaction systems. Why not operate a computer by speech if you do not want to use a keyboard, or by touching the monitor with a finger? One thing is certain, the first generation nerds and computer enthusiasts are being overtaken more and more by normal people who want to operate a computer as they once did a television: turn it on, choose a channel, and sit back and relax.

New User Interfaces, New Interactive Systems

What good is the best computer if it leaves you with a completely new, possibly totally confusing user interface after updating the system? Or a chic, shiny black MP3 player that can easily store unlimited numbers of CDs, but only has a tiny screen that displays illegible song titles? Or a menu tree that promises endless functions but is not user-friendly? "Handy ERGO," a study carried out by Gelsenkirchen Technical University in 2004, recorded devastating findings for information designers and engineers. "A disaster," according to the researchers. Even the participants, "who considered themselves experts, had an error margin of twenty-three percent. Beginners had a seventy-nine percent error margin when attempting to carry out a task." Of 1,200 subjects, a quarter failed to write a text message on two phones. The conclusion: "elementary requirements of software ergonomics such as suitability for the task, compatibility, and transparency are not fulfilled by modern mobile phones." [39]

39 Dahm, Markus; Felken, Christian; Klein-Bösing, Marc; Rompel, Gert; Stroick, Roman: "Handy ERGO: Breite Untersuchung über die Gebrauchstauglichkeit von Handys" (Mobile phone ERGO: a comprehensive study on the usability of mobile phones), in: Reinhard Keil-Slawik, Harald Selke, Gerd Szwillus (ed.): *Mensch & Computer 2004: Allgegenwärtige Interaktion* (Ubiquitous interaction). Oldenbourg, Munich, 2004, pp. 75—84; quoted in: http://mc.informatik.uni-hamburg.de/konferenzbaende/mc2004/mc2004_08_dahm_etal.pdf

40 In a dpa-Feature, quoted in http://www.nordbayern.de/dpa_art2.asp?art=779716&kat=8091&man=7 *

The study distinguished between age groups and concluded that human ability to adapt to new models begins declining at the age of thirty-one. The success rate declined to fifty-seven percent and, after the age of fifty, to thirty-seven percent. Psychology professor Hartmut Wandke of Berlin's Humboldt University states that on the whole, "seniors often feel overwhelmed by modern devices such as mobile phones." [40] And not only silver surfers turn off when they have to turn a device on — all age groups were dissatisfied. We are still years away from self-explanatory, even intuitive devices. To achieve this, the terminology must first be made consistent and standards have to be extended beyond obligatory norms. Academics at universities call for abandoning special methods for "consistency and compatibility beyond the manufacturers boundaries."

We need new user interfaces, new forms of interaction, and fortunately the largest companies in the field, Apple and Microsoft, are working precisely on these developments. Standing in line for hours or even

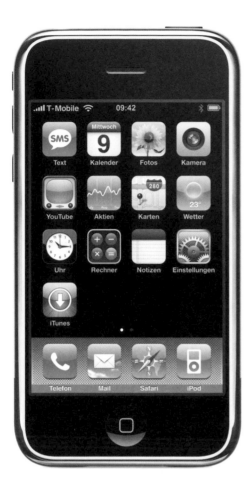

Apple iPhone
Mobile Phone by Apple

The revolutionary interface is a breakthrough in intuitive interaction between the user and the world. The principle of simplification was radically developed further and became a model for competitors.

just reading about the almost hysterical reactions to the market launch of **Apple's iPhone** revealed that many people harbor an unfulfilled desire to own a device that is both elegant and simple, and that can be used as a PDA (Personal Digital Assistant), videoplayer or simply a mobile phone.

At the least, Apple secured the usual lead in aesthetics — although it is still to be seen whether or not absolutely every user is truly 100 percent happy with the finger-controlled menu. Yet the idea is still impressive. Why not activate our primal method of pointing, the finger? Context controlled menus adapt to the human physiognomy, meaning that computers will no longer deform their users.

41 The console and its appearance online: http://de.wii.com/software/02/

A game console that reveals the future direction of interactive operation almost sounds like a joke: intuitive input, immediate feedback, an end to clicking a mouse, or shoving joysticks around, no more complicated keyboard combinations or long instructions. Wii sports convert real movements into virtual actions. [41] The slender console that recalls classic TV remote controls mutates into a tennis racket, a bowling ball, boxing gloves, a baseball bat, or a golf club. "This is what video games should be: fun for everyone!" according to Nintendo's promotional campaign. The game manufacturer not only caught the imagination of glassy-eyed players who did not want to sit down, it even reached the couch-potato generation of players.

Diverse manufacturers are opening the door for new interactions. Why not be able to enlarge windows on the monitor simply by moving your thumb and index finger apart, a function that Apple is developing now? Why not give people active control over things that define their lives, without forcing them to depend on limited input devices and user interfaces? The future of (entertainment) electronics has to be simplified if we wish to keep up with an increasingly complex world.

Microsoft's **Touchscreen Surface** has rediscovered the primal human activities of point, grasp, and move. It has developed a universal tabletop display on which entire groups of users can interactively surf, chat, and exchange information. There is no mouse or monitor; it is controlled purely with the hand. This is the next step in data processing that, suddenly using menus and scroll bars, makes something as self-evident and as tangible as it was before computers. As early as October 1999, the Fraunhofer Institute IPSI in Darmstadt presented a very similar concept called the "FOD_InteracTable®," which also combined table and

Roomware
Computer-augmented Room Elements by The Fraunhofer Institute IPSI, Darmstadt

As early as October 1999, developers demonstrated what interaction in the office place actually means: networked, programs that can be operated intuitively at different workstations and on different output media.

Touchscreen Surface
Tabletop Display by Microsoft

The end of the conventional desktop era is nigh. Images and data will be opened and organized by a movement of the hand. The computer will become a functional piece of room furniture.

42 Streitz, Norbert A.; Tandler, Peter; Müller-Tomfelde, Christian; Konomi, Shin'ichi: "Roomware. Towards the Next Generation of Human-Computer Interaction based on an Integrated Design of Real and Virtual Worlds." In: Carroll, John M. (ed.): *Human-Computer Interaction in the New Millennium*. Addison-Wesley, London, 2001, pp. 553—78.

display. Norbert Streitz, head of the research area "AMBIENTE — Arbeitswelten der Zukunft," [42] (Ambient — future work worlds) has studied user interfaces for decades. He speaks of a multilevel user pyramid: faster input for everyone, followed by the opportunity to optimize and personalize the environment as the pinnacle of the expert mode for the experienced user. His work was reflected in a series of innovations called **Roomware**® that connected real worlds with computer intelligence. User interfaces are no longer classified as the standardized outside edge of a main computer, they will be integrated in everyday objects — for instance in chairs such as the "FOD_CommChair®," podiums (ConnecTable®), and interactive information boards (DynaWall®). These can be interconnected and can simultaneously display information on different monitors that can be edited or processed at the same time. In addition to hardware, special programs will also play a core role. They make it possible, for instance, to move gestures of digital objects along a wall and to accompany this with sound. So-called "passengers" will be able to carry digital objects from one place, such as the DynaWall, to other Roomware components. The software will also enable several people to collaborate simultaneously and interactively on different Roomware components.

Let the future come, and with it a number of new connections between hard and software that accomplish something significant: they will serve the user, because objects will be intelligent.

They are everywhere. Pictograms call the shots in airport terminals, train stations, or business lounges. Stick figures and skirted ladies point the way to restrooms, crossed out cigarettes define no-smoking zones, zig-zag lines show the way to the stairs. No large international event can be held without the associated flood of information. Every escalator, taxi stand, or airport terminal needs a system of signs. Welcome to global culture. We are international, multicultural, flexible, and fast. Everything important needs to be immediately understood by everyone. Signs in German, English, and French are no longer enough. Pictograms are the signposts of international understanding. They are elaborate orientation systems that actually attempt to provide calm at moments when we are yet again frantically searching for our connecting flight, cannot find our gate, or locate a taxi stand. Because we are actually lost in the middle of a jungle of signs.

Critics scoffed at Otl Aicher's sports symbols for the 1972 Olympic games, calling them "a minimal written language for the illiterates of our hectic generation." The doyen of German graphic design worked six long years on the images. On sprinters that take off at forty-five degree angles, football players with a ball for a head, and marksmen that crawl along the ground in a line. Along what ground? Pictograms function by means of omission. The less there is to see, the better, or clearer, they are. Reading this degree of stylization has to be learned. Perhaps that is why the football player's head is displayed so obviously. The white ball sits so heavily on the torso that the athlete seems to raise his arms just to keep his head from falling off.

Aicher perfected a code that Japanese designers Masaru Katsumie and Yoshiro Yamashita developed in 1964 into a pictorial system of symbols representing different sports. This was achieved using very few bars and strokes. They bent arms at ninety-degree angles, concentrated on the torso, or marked the waist by omitting it — as well as maintaining a consistent weight and size of line as propagated by the Ulm Academy of Design. "Precise, dense, safe, nothing more to reduce, and moreover definitive," boasted Bernhard Rübenach of Ulm design. The symbols were accordingly sterile. The athletes themselves were elegant enough. The symbols merely had to be unmistakable.

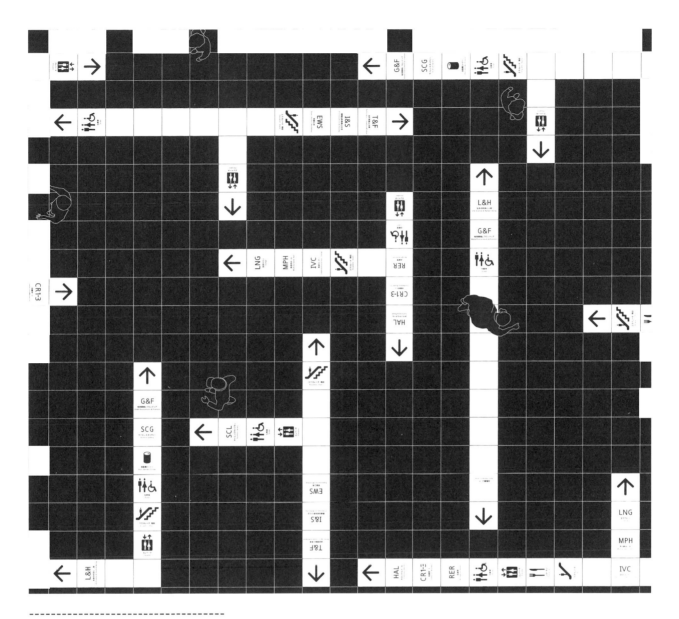

Walk-in Orientation System
National Science Museum in Tokyo
by Hiromura Design Office

Users go for it. Why not store information directly on the floor, where it can be immediately felt? The textured surface provides resistance and gives signals: Attention, Information. Please enter.

Helpful Signs

The Gutenberg galaxy feared competition from visual Steno. Are things so clear? Even a banal arrow can be misleading. Take, for instance, the Salzburg train station. Racing from track 21 to track 11 to catch the Vienna train can be a desperate endeavor for any traveler. It is almost impossible to tell if the arrow is pointing upwards, downwards, or straight ahead. Orientation systems fail in convoluted architecture and mutate into disorientation systems. Paul Mijksenaar, the sixty-one-year-old Dutch information designer, complains that even "the best orientation systems cannot help a flawed building." Schipol airport in Amsterdam, for which he developed the orientation system guidelines, is considered to be particularly user-friendly. The designer tackled the confusion of terminals and gates with an "easy-to-follow color code system and clear pictograms." He created a system. If the toilets are located directly above one another, Mijksenaar combined the arrows with a pictogram for stairs or escalators.

Precision is the key to visual information, yet context often plays an equally significant role in whether it is successful. For this reason, Fontshop, an alphabet construction kit for graphic designers and writers, makes an understatedly reserved bid for its pictograms: "They are excellent at communicating complicated messages in a clear and simple manner." In order to be understood, they must speak a clear visual language, work within a system that has the same syntax, and be formally consistent. That sounds like Erik Spiekermann, who years ago complained that, "this sign language can be considered a crude abbreviation of complex content." The famous typographer makes it very clear that, "symbolic illustrations cannot appear side by side with detailed technical images. Loosely drawn pictograms strategically distributed throughout a space speak a different language than extremely reduced symbols." We obviously have to work a bit more on our thoroughly designed world before information and transparency go hand in hand.

Losing the Way in the Forest of Signs

Today, however, there is a completely different problem. There are more and more signs competing in public space, with three large systems struggling for the lead: official pictograms, commercial advertisements, and graffiti. Unfortunately the first two are now adopting the subversive strategies of street art. Quantity is what counts: so-called bombing entails covering everything with spray paint, with posters, or with signs. Just to be noticed. And the result is disastrous. Many signs are little more than bad illustrations. They have no accountability. For example, there were two Americans recently in a Munich subway train who wanted to go to the zoo. They traced their finger along the map and could not find it. The public transportation system has commissioned a new subway map with gray sketches of tourist attractions such as the stadium, the zoo, and the town hall. But because no one knows what these mean yet, the word for them is added below each illustration. Real pictograms — that is extremely simplified pictorial signs — should not need to be repeated in written form.

Prohibitions can be excellently illustrated. A picture says no a thousand times, as traffic signs have shown. However, it took five international conventions between 1909 and 1968 before a consensus could be reached on a uniform system. Road signs are now permeating graphic design. The cigarette crossed through with a diagonal bar has had a successful career. It can be found in thousands of varieties. Balsa wood is not recommended for small children, so a baby is crossed out, as in a "restricted parking" space. "There used to be more time to read," Spiekermann complained about new signs. Today we have "a faceless pictogram with the simple message 'No children!' instead of detailed information on a prohibition."

It is not surprising that globalization loves pictograms. Time is money. America in particular is leading the way in standardization. The **AIGA** (American Institute of Graphic Arts), founded in 1914, offers fifty copyright-free signs and symbols that can be downloaded for free. The first thirty-four were launched in 1974 and were immediately awarded one of the first "Presidential Design Awards"; sixteen others were added in 1979. Today, all of America — from the immigration office to the last diner in Idaho — is adorned with coat hangers (checkrooms), telephone receivers (telephone booths), and banknotes (bureau de change). "This system of fifty symbol signs was designed for use at the crossroads of modern life: in airports and other transportation hubs and at large international events," according to AIGA. But what is the significance of this orientation system? "They are an example of how public-minded designers can address a universal communication need." That is correct. It is not a matter of a system of symbols for train passengers and globe-trotters; it is a matter of need. And sometimes it has to be fast. Where is the defibrillator? The symbol for a heart is immediately visible. Good graphic design can save lives.

Pictograms are a part of day-to-day life and are not the end of the written word. What would a billion Chinese people say? Their alphabet consists of abstract pictorial symbols. The A in its original form — upside down — was the symbol for cow. The horned steer head phonetically represented the animal: aleph. At one point a simple singular letter developed from the ideogram. Now the reverse is true. Today the cow represents a warning on the side of the road. We do not have to like the global society's new simplicity, but we do have to learn to read it. Because pictograms do not function alone. Only in conjunction with well-designed typography and well-placed information can they act as a visual compass in the thicket of a modern infrastructure in need of universal approaches.

Pictograms

Can be downloaded from AIGA:
http://www.aiga.org/content.cfm/
symbol-signs

Orientation System
Munich Airport by Wangler/Adele

Gather information and present it in a clear and concise manner. That is one aspect of the modern orientation system. Another aspect is integrating it into a given space and making it useable for all. These are the fundamental principles behind the award-winning orientation system at Munich Airport.

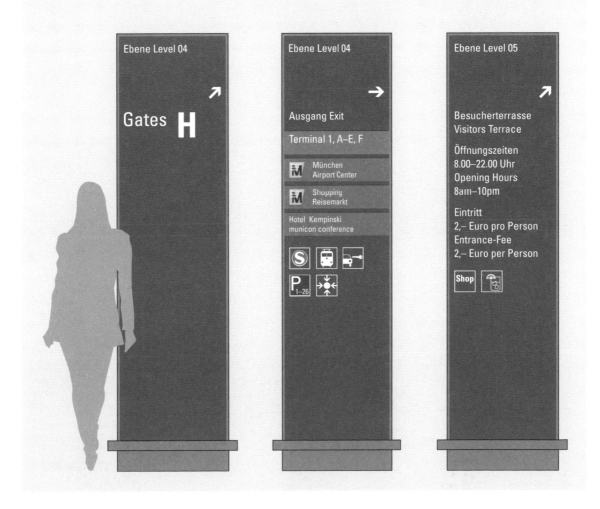

Designers Ursula Wangler and Frank Abele on Orientation
Systems in the Age of Universal Use

OH · **We live today in a thoroughly designed world. Information is amassing, is jumbled and confusing. How do you view this as a professional, visual person? And what does a normal person take in?**

FA · There are structures of relevance. An architect for instance concentrates on the built environment. One's perception is related to one's occupation, origins, and place of residence. We have to differentiate while designing: what makes the most sense for a certain target group, and what structure of perception does this target group possess?

UW · Perception is strongly related to context. Here's an example: we are traveling and have to change trains four times. Afterward, we have completely forgotten the architecture. We don't even know what the signs looked like. We only know that it worked and we arrived. Especially when pressed for time, it is difficult for people to convey content into decision.

OH · **Can you clarify this with an example?**

UW · A hospital, a large sign: Exit Left. Suddenly a woman approaches a group of doctors and asks where the exit is. The chief physician points to the sign above that reads, loud and clear, Exit Left. One could assume the woman had read the sign. Yet she was still momentarily overwhelmed. There has to be a basic readiness to absorb the available information.

FA · There are different preferences. Generally, young people use interactive communication means while older people often reject this in favor of relying on architecture or addressing a person directly. Others refer to maps. Different structures of perception need to be conveyed in different ways that should all be used strategically.

UW   They should all also be applied — from the classic site plan to the interactive program.

OH   **You're shooting a bit in the dark as soon as there's no homogenous target group. How does a universal orientation system function, for example at an airport?**

UW   The most important information is about the destination: where do I need to go? To terminal one or terminal two? This information must first exist in printed form, a map, or a ticket. This information helps a person make a decision. Then you can use any media, from GPS, to a site plan, or just ask. It will never be possible to forego personal information, which can alleviate aggression and insecurity.

FA   Places need to be marked with signs. Today, we need more than an elevator with signs containing information about all the different levels. As soon as the doors open, the information has to appear again right there where the traveler is.

UW   Our memory capacity is limited. We need constant confirmation.

What Constitutes a Good Orientation System?

OH   **A good orientation system is redundant. How redundant does it have to be at an airport?**

UW   Very redundant. And it has to be constructed in such a way as to reduce the number of destination possibilities to the absolute minimum.

OH   **For example?**

UW   There have to be orientation systems leading to the gates, and then to the specific gates like H—J, then to numbers 1—24, and 25—48. Then you go to the individual gate.

The orientation system at Munich
Airport is a key for all who need to
find their way between the gates.

FA   They also have to lead first to the exits and not to the taxis, buses, or rental cars. Our ability to absorb information is limited, as is our ability to hold a mental picture of everything except the main destinations that will always reappear. That is how redundancy should function.

OH   **Is there a hierarchy between text and color?**
FA   Language is in the foreground, it is rational.

UW   Color offers support. However this has little to do with the color itself, but rather with contrast.

FA   But we believe that too much contrast ends up problematic.

OH   **There are more and more retail shops at airports that passengers are forced to walk past. Does that not conflict with the need for transparency regarding the orientation systems? It's almost impossible to make a decision in this case. I have to walk by these shops, whether I want to or not.**
UW   As far as we are concerned, information is the priority. Yet we have developed concepts where the flow of information is actually halted. An announcement is made about when to go to the gate and how much time is needed to get there. The system is not designed to get the passenger to the gate as soon as possible, but offers dynamic information about how far the gate is.

OH   **So if it takes fifteen minutes to get to the gate, I'll go directly to the gate. But if it only takes three-minutes to get there, can I still buy something on the way?**
UW   That is also decision-making assistance.

FA   It always depends on the site. I'd rather take my time in a museum, but not in an airport.

OH   **How are architecture and orientation systems related? You said it is best if an orientation system does not have to compete with the architecture.**

UW   An orientation system or any interactive system always has to be anchored in the architecture. It is best if we can plan together with the architects.

OH   **How often does that happen?**

UW   In our case relatively often because we are involved in many new projects.

FA   We don't see our work as being separate. Our work serves the architecture.

OH   **So you approach a specific site and its unique qualities. Does that not conflict with the requirements of universal orientation systems?**

UW   I don't believe that. You can't even find a universal orientation system on the Internet, where they would be so easy to embed. We live in Europe where we have a tradition of the individual, the region, and of different cultures. There would otherwise be no need for new architecture. There are already enough highly optimized hospitals, yet we still continue to announce new competitions anyway.

OH   **So you design for Europe. Can you afford to do this in terms of an airport?**

UW   Individuality also provides orientation. The traveler knows for example that he or she has arrived in Munich, a high-quality airport. It has a bright and quiet atmosphere that is very conducive to orientation. However, hotels are quite the opposite. You don't know where you are. Individuality in a design concept is important: it must be tailored to the site, the company, the target group.

| OH | **Meaning the universal becomes less important than the site?** |
| UW | The universal is important in pictograms. But there are cultural differences here as well. |

| FA | Orientation systems are enduring. They are a part of architecture and cannot afford to be trendy. They should be independent and transport content. Content provides the bridge, the access. |

| UW | They will however never be completely timeless. A good design always reveals the age it comes from. We do things differently today. |

The Future is Exciting

| OH | **Do you mean, we design better? Is experience a value regarding orientation systems?** |
| UW | Experience is a value, but I meant that the environment has changed; techniques have changed. As well as the information that is available. Address books have become obsolete; this information can be recorded more successfully on the Internet. Using various media at the same time offers the opportunity to direct information. |

| OH | **There is a new drive to provide specific information tailored to individual users. How does that function?** |
| FA | In the hospital, for example, the computer will recognize who is standing in front of its monitor. The nursing staff, doctors, and visitors see different content-related information. Ideally, only the necessary information will appear. On the other hand, this could get out of control. |

| OH | **Meaning the individual could become incapacitated through technology?** |
| FA | Withholding information could be seen as incapacitating. Which is why we try to avoid this. |

OH   **To sum up, can you say how design will have to change, considering our society is getting increasingly older? Is it enough just to make the print larger?**

UW   That's compulsory. No one will read if it's too much effort. With regard to information acquisition, every generation has been influenced and will carry these values with them into old age.

OH   **HiFi compared to WiFi?**

UW   For example.

FA   The gap between the generations is closing. Lifestyle and structures of perception are opening up.

OH   **That means that target groups will become more diffuse. Does that mean that it will be more difficult to design?**

FA   Yes.

UW   It will definitely get more difficult, and this is made worse by a decline in education: there will be great differences. People who will not be able to understand clear analog or interactive information. That will be a challenge for design and it may decline in comparison to today's standards.

EAR

Surround Sound Eyewear
Design by Industrial Facility

A better way of hearing in the most beautiful form: invisible.

HEARING WELL IS THE FIRST STEP TO LIVING WELL.

PLUTARCH

Ear

It might not be our most essential organ but it is indispensable neverthe-less. Hearing is also speaking, maintaining a dialog with a community that is rooted in exchange. A person who is unable to participate in this com-munication is ostracized; anyone with even a temporary hearing problem will confirm this.

A picture is supposed to say a thousand words, yet one single word is enough to either exasperate or completely delight someone. Recent advancements in microelectronics, new sensor technology, and adaptable software have drastically improved the comfort and aesthetics of hearing aids over the last few years. They are no longer a stigmatizing device or a sign of disability, but are high-tech miniatures that can adapt to both the environment and their wearers. Yet they will only be dealt with periph-erally in this context as an all-in-one instrument. The reason is simple. As pleasant as they are, they can still only target a certain group. Those keeping up with the times will demand more general solutions, even Universal Designs that have escaped the niche of special applications and deficits, and have begun to open doors for everyone.

Modern Crossover: Glasses that Hear

A pair of glasses that can hear? Sounds like one of Q's gadgets for James Bond. But they are now reality. Despite the fact that today's hearing aids have made great technical and aesthetic advances, they still evoke the idea of a handicap, an impairment, and remain a more or less visible compensation for disability. Yet no one considers glasses to be a sign of weakness; they are too common as everyday objects, fashion, a fleeting lifestyle, and as the staging of a moment.

43 The designer's statement is crys-tal clear: "Hearing glasses have existed before. They disappeared primarily be-cause of the combination of two func-tions that were articulated in an awkward, incohesive and problematic manner. Instead, 'Surround Sound Eye-wear' attempts to create a more holistic object not intended to hide the hearing aid, but to incorporate it gracefully."

Maybe that was the driving force behind Sam Hecht and Kim Colin's idea to strip away the last stigma from hearing aids and to integrate them visibly into glasses. But there is more than that. The long-standing problematic relationship between designers and multifunctional devices [43] promises to ease forever with **Surround Sound Eyewear** by Industrial Facility because it offers added value. The hearing glasses were created in

Surround Sound Eyewear
Glasses by Industrial Facility

Three-dimensional hearing is concealed in a pair of glasses. British designers Sam Hecht and Kim Colin have made it possible—innovations in collaboration with the London Royal National Institute for the Deaf (RNID).

2005 for the London Royal National Institute for Deaf People (RNID). Sam Hecht and Kim Colin concentrated on more than just the social and aesthetic aspects, they brought the ability to hear to new heights by placing four microphones on each side. They based their design on the research by Professor Marinus Boone of Delft University. The designers from Industrial Facility claim that "the result is a type of 3 dimensional superhuman hearing similar to that found in certain animals such as coyotes." A better way of hearing in the most beautiful form: invisible. What could be better for the second most important human information organ?

Size Alone Does Not Matter: Mobile Phones on the Road to Becoming an Ergonomic Product

Few other products can boast such a high level of acceptance and market saturation. Italy and Germany have statistically more mobile phones than people. The flip side of the mobile phone's fabulous success is an equally short story. No other technical invention so quickly changed its category from status symbol, to practical object, to fashion item. We buy mobile telephones today to match our wardrobe. They come with a built-in expiration date; they barely go into production before their technical features become outmoded. Even people with the most rudimentary knowledge of the mobile phone market and its particularly cryptic abbreviations (UMTS, roaming, SMS) know how short-lived these products are. And technical features are no longer a guaranteed sales pitch, giving way to "soft" features such as haptics, aesthetics, and design.

Ergonomics and handling are growing in significance. Small

displays, tricky convoluted menus, and tiny buttons might have been sexy as innovative design, but are in fact weaknesses in design, which, called styling, are often created to fit one identically built group, like a mantle over a black box called technology.

Yet user-friendliness will soon become an important sales promotion criterion when paired with equally attractive aesthetics. Products with a recognizably simple design will be little more than shelf warmers if their technical features are not convincing. The iPod phenomenon has proved that an ingeniously simple operating system together with the newest advancements in technology will guarantee success. A mobile phone for the older generation should not be recognized as such, nor should it expose its wearer as an old person or even draw attention to the fact. Senior design quickly becomes discriminatory design, which is considered an area of special products produced in small series and not equipped with the newest features. Scanning the market for devices that suit all generations reveals two basic strategies: simplification via size and/or via concentrating on less functional elements.

· Simplification by enlargement means that everything will be bigger: keyboards, buttons, menus, and the case or box. Aesthetics often get lost along the way, while the ergonomics and operating system are not actually improved. Inflated, oversized appliances are quickly put in the rehabilitation context, and branded as crude, awkward, and ugly.

· Simplification via reduction on the other hand often means omitting whatever you can. Reducing features deeply affects user routines and standards. The three-button mobile phone (on, off, emergency call) will quickly end up in both an aesthetic and technical dead end of special products.

Both methods are problematic. Simplicity should be at the fore, but not simplification. Ergonomics should set the standard, and not a blown-up version of a normal mobile phone. Apparently, designers and engineers are still scratching the surface of ergonomic appliances instead of developing a fundamentally new mobile phone construction. What conclusions can be drawn from this? That combining ergonomics and aesthetics promises success. Konstantin Grcic outlines the fascinating area of

Emporia Voice
Universal Cell Phone by Emporia

You will know it by its easy-to-handle design. A new generation of cell phones is attempting to make operating a cell phone as simple and as intuitive as possible, without making the phones look like objects for the old and frail.

sensible reduction in the following interview and prescribes urges designers to use intelligence, or more precisely: he calls for intelligent things that make users truly more intelligent. This is exactly where the issue of ergonomics comes into play, in regard to how a sensible reduction of contemporary complexity might look. Critical user reports have long sounded like surrenders to the technically feasible and easily marketed. **BAGSO** (German National Association of Senior Citizens' Organizations) recommends the following: "Do not be concerned with functions that initially seem unnecessary (such as language, camera, radio), you may want to use these later. It is first important to master the functions you need right away." [44] The instructions for operating appliances sound like a summary of Universal Design principles, like a check list for more than mobile phones: [45]

44 *Nutzerfreundliche Produkte. Leicht bedienbar und Generationengerecht* (User-friendly products. Easy to use and generation friendly). BAGSO, n.d., p. 5; http://www.bagso.de/fileadmin/Aktuell/Broschuere_Nutzerfreundliche_Produkte.pdf *

45 *Nutzerfreundliche Produkte*, p. 5. *

- "Check to make sure the mobile phone fits neatly in the hand (form, material, weight).
- Look for a logical, clear arrangement of the keys.
- All keys should be illuminated and large enough to operate comfortably and precisely — with a clearly discernable counter pressure in the keys. A touchtone provides audible support (can be deactivated).
- In low light conditions or in the event of visual impairments, the number 5 should have an added textured surface, and individual keys should in general be easily distinguished by touch.
- Letters and symbols should be easily legible and simple to understand.
- Mobile phones are much easier to use if you are able to answer incoming calls by pushing any button (settings).
- In the case of a clamshell mobile phone, sliding the device open answers incoming calls.
- A large display is an advantage.
- The information in the display should be large enough, with enough contrast to be legible in different lighting conditions. It is practical if the foreground and background can be adjusted. The display should not reflect glare."

An ergonomic and easy to operate mobile telephone requires clear visuals, doubled symbolicity or repetition for important functions (signal beyond sound and image), good haptic quality, and logical menu navigation. Even the youngest generations fail to operate appliances that are overloaded with functions. A good example here is the grandfather of development: the **BasicPhone** designed by npk (headed by Jos Oberdorf and Hans Antonissen) and commissioned by Totaal 2005. The phone cannot be compared to today's telephone technology and its capabilities, but the Dutch designers valued reduction and only a few functions that could be operated well: an ergonomic body, an adjustable loudspeaker function, large symbols on the keys, but no SMS function. BasicPhone offers exactly what its name promises: it is in effect an emergency phone that successfully combines simplicity and clarity. Yet two details reveal that convincing solutions still need to be developed: important saved phone numbers can be written on the reverse side of the phone, and the phone can be worn on a band around the neck, so that the wearer always knows where it is. Technology in the future will have to depend less on improvisation.

In spite of skepticism, mobile telecommunication is developing into a key field of modern product development and cross-generation research. Telecommunication provides an interface with the modern world. Only those who participate in communication remain a core part of life and can, if necessary, call for help. A market for ergonomic products exists for the first time. In Germany alone, there are a good dozen appliances available, even more if emergency telephones are included in this figure. Their names are **Secufone, Simplephone, Katharina das Große, Easy2, Emporia**, and Co. Yet sometimes, good intentions seem to precede good design. Problems occur with overly convoluted menus, or if the device is awkward to handle, the keys do not provide enough feedback, the sliding mechanism is problematic, or if an older, larger hand has difficulties opening the lower or upper cover with one movement.

Ultimately, the development of this field revolves around a core question that makes mobile telephones all the more interesting: how can advanced technology be designed in a sensible manner? It is more than just large display screens, fewer technical knickknacks or reduced functions — it is really an issue of finally reconciling design and ergonomics.

Cell Phones

The ethics and aesthetics of telecommunications

They should be easy to use, have a large display and accessible menus — and not just be an inflated standard device. Here pictured: EmporiaLIFE.

Developing the Perfect Cell Phone

The market of so-called senior telephones is getting more and more crowded: Big Easy, EmporiaTIME, and Basic Phone demonstrate today's extent of technology and design.

MAYDAY

Lamp by Konstantin Grcic for Flos

The lamp for everyone: simple, universal, and most likely with the longest cable on the planet.

Designer Konstantin Grcic on experienced designers,
enduring products, and the art of reduction

OH   **You were celebrated as a young star for so long that you seemed glad to finally get rid of that label. How do you feel today, in your early forties?**

KG   I actually feel free, because that label was never totally correct in the first place. Young stars today are sixteen to twenty-four years of age and are often still quite naïve. Back then, I already had an academic education behind me and no longer belonged to that age group. Regardless: that is the past. I am older now, the office has grown, and we are all more experienced. We're working on a more advanced level, which gives me a lot more opportunities, more experience, and competence. I could never have done Chair_ONE back then …

OH   **… because of technology, your newly won experience, or the radical approach that you have developed?**

KG   Everything together. I've outgrown the beginnings. At the moment I feel that what we are doing has developed of itself and that it's good. This awareness gives me the confidence to continue on my own path.

OH   **You have developed a very special design language. One key issue seems to be reduction. Can that help to design things for the over-sixty and over-seventy generation?**

KG   A difficult question. It will be impossible to compare the future older generation to our elderly today. The former can use computers, digital media, and can get around today's sensory overload. This makes them more intellectually fit and they will also have learned to reinvent themselves at regular intervals. They will be more flexible.

OH **You talk about the old elderly of today and the young elderly of tomorrow. You also speak about ignoring or reducing sensory overload. Again, is that a challenge to design?**

KG Simplification is a fundamental issue. It does not mean however that something has to be taken away from artifacts. I have become very critical about this. Simplification often leads to banality and damages our relationship to the artifact. We always need some emotional connection to objects, and this is where designers find their greatest challenge: giving the object an essence.

Design Should Make Users Intelligent

OH **So, is reduction a pointless principle?**

KG That depends. When an artifact loses its essence, then reduction has gone too far. It is more about sensible differences. When is an object simple, when is it complex? And, what is an intelligent object? Something that educates me, that gives me control. Too many buttons can degrade a person into someone who doesn't understand. The iPod is a favorite example here because it can be operated intuitively, or the iPhone. I was in America last summer ...

OH **... and went shopping?**

KG No, but tried them out. The user interface is very complex, yet intuitive. That's the direction we need to go.

OH **That is what representatives of Universal Design would say: intuitive, simple, and redundant. Does that appeal to you?**

KG Of course. What we do is check things again and again. Intuition is essential. Users should be able to navigate an object immediately. Older people are agile and will remain so.

OH **Should design challenge the user?**

KG That is very important. There are thirty-year-olds who have already begun to lose agility. A simplification of design should not encourage that further.

OH	You want to bring design to the point without simplifying it. At the same time you support barrier-free access.

OH You want to bring design to the point without simplifying it. At the same time you support barrier-free access.

KG That's correct. Breaking down barriers and involving people immediately and introducing them to the world.

OH Would it be a challenge to develop a phone for a seventy-year-old that would also appeal to a thirty-year-old?

KG That would in fact be very valuable, because you could filter out certain functions that have nothing to do with age. A friend in Tokyo bought a phone designed for the elderly and he is thirty. The telephone doesn't look like much. But he liked exactly the non-design aspect of it, because all the other phones look either very sporty, organic, or technical.

Make It Simpler!

OH What do the manufacturers think? Do they have something against the simple?

KG Designers are always saying: make it simpler, no one will use that. Simple functions, at least on the surface. Fanatics can use anything, but it is essential to reduce things and make them simple.

OH Why does that so often fail? Do the engineers always call the shots and pack another ten functions into everything?

KG It's not the engineers, it's marketing. The sales situation is brutal today. There are twenty appliances standing in a row. The first decision is price-related, then technology-related. The more functions a consumer can buy for the money the better. Regarding design, this means the more buttons the better, and the market has corrupted this. The negative aspect is marketing, the sales manipulation.

OH Does Apple then have a particularly good or a particularly bad marketing concept?

KG That is a phenomenon. People are now willing to pay more money for quality goods. The fact that there are still so few competitors shows that this is a difficult direction. It is easier to over pack the surface with functions and to install a lighting console. Simplicity is suddenly very complex and connected with extensive research, which industry cannot afford at the moment. Everyone wants a low risk product — meaning, the shortest development time possible, fast products, short product cycles, in order to hopefully gain a piece of the market. The next one is already waiting at the door. The culture of short-lived technological products will surely end soon. I think that technological development in the future will become more gradual. This could mean that industry will be able to develop new forms and things that consumers can possess for a longer period of time.

OH **Durable goods for consumers who will become older?**

KG That is precisely what makes a person feel secure: knowing something and using it for a long time. I see this as an interesting aspect and why wouldn't it be appealing to a thirty-year-old. This idea gives hope for a market that has become insane. Sometimes there are products that are well-engineered and technically mature. In this case, it's important to let them stay on the market as they are. What is better than a successful product? Suddenly, it's possible to concentrate on details, instead of always creating something new.

Adhesive plaster dispenser
Design by Wolf Jeschonnek

It couldn't be easier: rip it off
and that's it!

FOR IN USING CLUBS AND
FLINTS, THEIR HANDS HAD
DEVELOPED A DEXTERITY
FOUND NOWHERE ELSE
IN THE ANIMAL KINGDOM,
PERMITTING THEM TO
MAKE STILL BETTER TOOLS,
WHICH IN TURN HAD
DEVELOPED THEIR LIMBS
AND BRAINS YET FURTHER.
IT WAS AN ACCELERATING,
CUMULATIVE PROCESS;
AND AT ITS END WAS MAN.

ARTHUR C. CLARKE

Hand

Manageable, palpable, tangible. Our vocabulary overflows with homage to our hands, which have helped us to seize and dominate the world. Over the course of a lifetime we learn that sensation in our fingertips is important when we use something, that surface structure reveals much about an object, and that often the right skill can be the decisive factor in the success of packaging. There are standardized answers for standard questions; but there are appropriate solutions for packaging problems. The world functions well as long as we can twist, peel, cut, pull, or break off, unravel, dismantle, unlock, tear, turn on, uncork, unlatch, unbolt, or open. Is that all? Or are there simpler, more enlightening and clearer solutions for using things? Our world may indeed be the best of all possible worlds, but it is also what we make of it, or what we draw from it. The greatest inventions in packaging history were either simply engineering solutions (guaranteed without the help of designers) or great achievements such as the crown cap or the staple. Yet this does not imply that standard solutions cannot still be improved. Things have to be easier to use in the future. Expert knowledge needs to be translated into practical simplicity, especially if society as a whole is getting older. Besides everything changes during our lifetimes, including changes in our motor abilities that vary considerably from individual to individual. Our limbs are not as flexible, we cannot twist our torsos as far, or bend our hips as much; we have to hold on to something to keep our balance, and our sense of touch diminishes as well. And once again: in an attempt to compensate for deficits, design should not stigmatize its users but should open environments and enable activities that would otherwise be challenging or too difficult to access or perform. Reconciling ergonomics and aesthetics is a challenge to all designers.

If you believe design is a creation myth, or a titanic effort of human Demiurges who want to create new worlds, reflect on the great entirety, or minutely analyze and completely organize every last detail from the city to the teaspoon — then skip this chapter. This chapter focuses on the small details, or on improvements in detail, comparable to a swimmer who has achieved an elegant turn, who has optimized his or her technique and succeeds due to the sum of individual optimization processes. It takes time to see whether many small changes have grown into a profound transformation whose outcome has little to do with the source. The motto is, "Learn from the home improvement store" — not in the sense of the superficial, oft cheaply thrown together house extension aesthetic, but as an incentive that turns people into the designers of their own environments and that dispels their fears and inhibitions. Our world needs efficient members who can do the job. Yet, if even simple can openers mutate into huge appliances, into special products for a precisely defined target group with disabilities, or if ergonomic knowledge is ignored and function becomes little more than a crutch, then designers are requested to return the task of aesthetics and general usability to the engineers.

It's All in the Packaging

Packaging sets the tone. There is hardly a product that is not sealed in foil, vacuum-packed, or at least wrapped several times so it maintains form, color, and taste (in the case of food) despite transportation. Outer packaging is mostly made of plastic, metal, wood, or biodegradable material. What about the manageability of individual products and their packaging solutions? A representative survey of 350 consumers carried out by BAGSO (German National Association of Senior Citizens' Organizations) in 2003 recorded devastating findings. [46] It looks bad for packaging quality: sixty-six percent of those surveyed complained that the expiration date was difficult to read, a further fifty-six percent said that the writing is too small or difficult to read, and another thirty-six percent criticized that packaging provides too little information about content. And another important aspect: sixty-four percent of those surveyed complained that packaging was difficult or impossible to open. The question was then formulated more specifically: how often is it impossible to open packaging at the first attempt? The reaction was devastating: an astonishing eight percent had to wrestle with packaging on a day-to-day basis. A total of ninety-two percent admitted having problems, forty-one percent even several times a week, twenty-seven percent once a week, and eighteen percent once a month.

Statistics differentiate between age and the type of packaging, however the figures are telling: it means there is no compensating factor for the few over-eighty-year-olds. Foil-sealed products are the most problematic for all generations (73.3 percent complained about foil

46 *Beschwerdepool für ältere Verbraucher. Ergebnisse der Befragung zum Thema Verpackungen* (Grievance platform for older consumers. The results of a survey about packaging), BAGSO, 2003. Cited from: http://www.bagso.de/fileadmin/Verbraucherforum/Verpackungen_01.pdf

Sausage Casing
Packaging by Gesa Nolte

The solution to an age-old problem: how can sausage best be apportioned? The young designer developed a fascinating answer: just unwrap it!

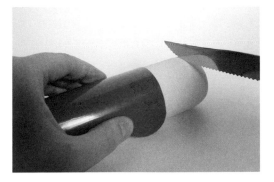

packaging), but also milk cartons (39.2 percent), coffee (30.7 percent), tin cans (28 percent), beverage bottles (27.4 percent), jam jars and cleaning agents (24.3 percent), yoghurt and white cheese (15.5 percent), and pharmaceutical products (14.6 percent). All other products groups were assessed as an overall 15.8 percent. Consumerism — made difficult. Over half of these customers, that is fifty-seven percent, changed brands, while forty percent thought packaging "is unnecessary for certain foods, body care products, and cosmetics."

Gesa Nolte, a twenty-two-year-old design student at the Braunschweig University of Art, created a practical **packaging for sausage** made of synthetic casing by drawing conclusions based on these devastating findings. A "particular release coating" in the casing allows it to be cleanly pealed off the sausage. The casing continues to function as packaging even after opening. It comes with a 4.5-centimeter long cap that provides product details such as ingredients, weight, manufacturer, and price. For safety, the expiration date is printed directly on the synthetic casing. It is divided into a series of tabs, each three centimeters wide, which can be easily pealed off to uncover enough meat for one or two pieces of bread. Clean slices. Afterwards you can place the cardboard lid over the open end. The sausage can be stored in an upright or horizontal position in the refrigerator until the next snack.

47 Schmidt-Ruhland, Karin (ed.): *Pack ein — pack aus — pack zu. Neue Verpackungen für Alt und Jung.* Berlin University of the Arts, 2006. *

Nolte's design was awarded distinction in the nationwide competition "Pack ein — pack aus — pack zu. Neue Verpackungen für Alt und Jung" (Pack in — pack out — take hold. New packaging for the old and young). [47]

The brief simply stated: "Is it possible to envisage product packaging that takes the needs of older people into consideration without its design and function being limited to this one user group?" Universal Design principles are displayed in the **adhesive plaster dispenser** by Wolf Jeschonnek. If good design is often the result of minute modifications, then this solution is particularly charming. Life's objects find their way to users and also become part of their infrastructure. Adhesive plaster will no longer be packed away in the first aid box, but can be where ever the user needs it: in the kitchen, the bathroom, the office, or quickly hung on a door handle. Packaging is reduced to the minimum. A piece of plaster can be removed with one hand and applied to a wound without a lot of effort. Innovation can be so simple. Jeschonnek, a student at the

Dremi
Design by Sang Woo Lee

A knife makes it a cinch to open the lid.

Quando
Fasteners by Meike Langer

Plastic clip for freezer bags: Memo
assistance and packaging fasteners
in one.

Weissensee School of Art and Design in Berlin, was awarded first prize for his design for the 2006 national competition.

48 Schmidt-Ruhland, Karin (ed.): *Pack ein — pack aus — pack zu. Neue Verpackungen für Alt und Jung* Berlin University of the Arts, 2006.

Natali Pilic, Catherina Borowitza, Sang Woo Lee, and Meike Langer want to know. Every prizewinner and shortlisted designer in the above-mentioned competition [48] tackled the issue of packaging and addressed a problem that emerges again and again: how can today's product world be simplified, how can food be better transported, better packed, and dispensed? The significance of the principle of leverage theory is not a coincidence. Natali Pilic and Catherina Borowitza make use of oversized screw tops; **triangular fasteners** and **wing-headed fasteners** accommodate the hand and make bottles easier to open by improving the transmission of power. Sang Woo Lee uses a trick for his series of **colorful caps** and adds protruding grip enhancements. If nothing else works, the user can stick a kitchen knife into special slots under the cap. The jar can then be easily opened using a bit of leverage. The large number of student works incorporating color codes, grip enhancements, and intelligent simplicity make it clear that the issue of packaging and wrapping is still in great need of improvement. **Quando**, Meike Langer's multifunctional product, goes much further. It offers optical memo assistance and packaging in one. Instead of having to decode the handwritten labels on the food we freeze, the date can be set on a scale. A plastic clip hermetically seals the freezer bag.

It is no wonder that even large companies are now compelled to be innovative. Hanno Kortleven designed a series of oval storage containers for Tupperware with easy-to-open lids, which enable foods to be transferred directly from the freezer to the microwave. Small feet on the bottom allow heat to totally surround the container when the box is heated up to 160 degrees from as low as twenty-five. When **Heat N Serve** is put into the microwave, a special silicon vent lets steam escape and promotes even heating. Form and material help develop multifunctional objects. The storage container is on the way to becoming a universal, easy-to-use storage and kitchen appliance.

Packaging is everything today: it is a tactile sales area, it attracts attention, and it serves as a protective shell and covering; at the same time it is also a three-dimensional user interface for objects that want to unfold before our eyes and make an impact. For a long time it primarily served industry and particularly marketing and sales while ergonomic requirements were largely ignored. That will and must change if everyone in the future is to enjoy products that fulfill all users' desires and needs.

Heat N Serve
Freezer Container by Hanno Kortleven for Tupperware

The form makes it easy to use. The material makes it multi-functional.

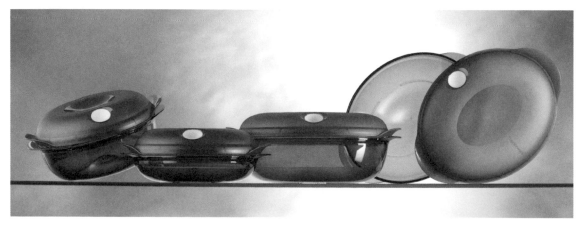

Wing-shaped Bottle Cap
Study by Catherina Borowitzka

The ergonomic wing-shaped cap
makes bottles easier to open.

Open Sesame

Packaging by Dési Doell,
ddddesign, Berlin

Easy-to-open beverage container thanks
to an integrated flap that a second bottle
can activate as a lever.

Carry on

Beverage Case by Dési Doell,
ddddesign, Berlin

Everything under control. The handle
located in the center of the beverage
case is also a bottle opener.

Heilbronner
Screw-cap by Natali Pilic

This ergonomic bottle cap is designed for maximal grip and transmission of power.

Rolling

Inspired by fruit. An apple supposedly inspired Sir Isaac Newton to explore the phenomenon of gravity. Yet Martin Hauenstein did not become a legend when, one autumn, he decided to carry a lemon tree up a flight of stairs to bring it inside for the winter, and then to bring it back down the stairs and outside on the terrace again in the spring. "A very difficult task," says the Munich-based designer, "which inspired me to design a device that would make the job easier. Because, even people under fifty don't want a broken back." The principle is as simple as it is convincing. The ladder doubles as a guiding rail for a movable sliding carriage that can transport a load upward or downward. Hauenstein made a sketch illustrating his lemon tree being transported downward on the diagonal ladder via a conveyor belt. It is both energy efficient and gentle on the back. The concept was convincing and within two weeks Hailo, a ladder manufacturer, produced a prototype that could then be optimized by designers and manufacturers. A handle was added so that the guiding rail could also double as a separate dolly on which an article could be transported to the **ladder conveyor**. The ladder can be extended along the floor on feet equipped with non-slip talons, and it therefore guarantees a secure position even on sloping terrain. The ladder lift can transport heavy loads upward or downward as safely as if on a pulley. Colorful ropes indicate where one needs to pull. Simple, effective details form a work tool that can adapt to different situations and help people.

The principle is simple: combine tried and tested elements. Maike Ahler's **rolling beverage case** does just this but in a rather astounding manner. A standard beverage case is equipped with wheels, such as those on rolling suitcases we see at airports. The motto here is "no more carrying." Instead of having to lug around bottles, the shopping itself becomes a wagon to transport the goods home. To do this, all users have to do is pull out the retractable grip and be on their way. It is an interesting solution that can serve as an example.

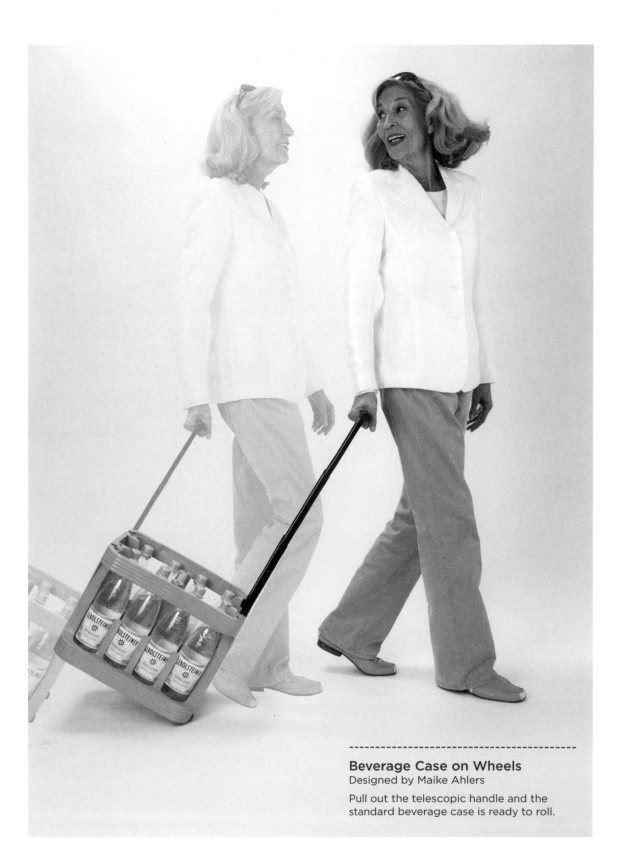

Beverage Case on Wheels
Designed by Maike Ahlers

Pull out the telescopic handle and the standard beverage case is ready to roll.

Pullmann 50
Ladder Conveyor by Martin Hauenstein
for Hailo

Sketches and realization. A sliding carriage
safely transports loads upward or downward.

Grasping

Tools were definitive in the development of humans. In order to take possession of the world one has to be able to change it, particularly the man-made environment. Something always needs to be tightened or loosened, attached or disconnected. And it is essential that the tip of a tool fits with precision and is easy to manage. Wiha's ergonomic **Inomic pliers** generation was created in collaboration with the Institut für Arbeitswirtschaft und Organisation (IAO) (Institute for Industrial Engineering) in Stuttgart and has already been awarded both the 2007 iF Product Design Award and the red dot design award — and not only because the device boasts an innovative and ergonomic form as well as precision manufacturing. The plier tips have been precisely manufactured using a new technology called metal injection molding, or MIM. A tiny slot in the surface distinguishes these from standard pliers. The tips are angled by twenty-three degrees to allow for optimal grip on any object. Fingers, ligaments, and muscles in the hand remain relaxed. The pliers are also able to convey twenty-five percent more force than conventional designs. But what is force without precision and exact application?

It is incorrect to assume that banal objects such as the **nutcracker** cannot be improved. Rösle's iF winning model is an innovation that abandons symmetry and consistency in design. Two differently shaped halves grasp a nut between pincers with so much force that diagonally extended prongs have a secure grip on their prey. Since only the pincers convey the force, the shell is cracked without destroying the flesh of the nut. Less exertion — Universal Design pervades even the smallest corners.

The knife may well be the ultimate tool, even more so than the screwdriver or hammer. It has accompanied humans for thousands of years and is now being tamed. When the Smart Design team was planning to develop the OXO Good Grips **Utility knife**, it not only met with the challenge of elegantly packaging the extra blades, but also of creating a guaranteed safe tool out of the familiar, handy carpet knife. First they fitted a large handle onto the base of the standard design that makes it easier to grip the casing and can also store extra blades safely. When the casing is opened, a reservoir for blades unfolds that allows the extra blades to be removed safely. Close the cover, lock it in place, and you are done. Two principles were essential while developing the design: safety and convenience, from fail-safe handling to the ergonomic handle that is designed to withstand force.

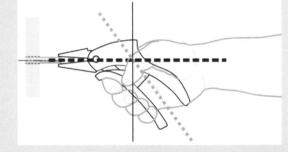

Top
Panic Exit Device by Dhemen Design for Tesa

Opens quickly even in the dark. The American principle, enhanced through design.

Inomic
Pliers manufactured by Wiha

The inclined handle allows maximal transmission of power and ensures a strong grip.

365+
Bread Knife by Ergonomidesign
for Ikea

Even arthritic joints can cut bread with
this knife. The tilted handle makes it
possible.

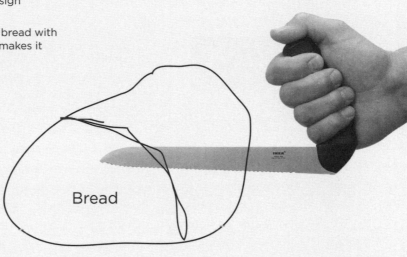

Bread

Nutcracker
Manufactured by Rösle

The asymmetrically held nutcracker transmits
power exactly where you need it. It crushes
the nutshell, not its contents.

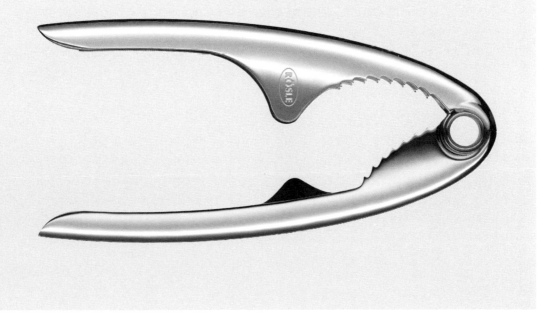

Swedish designers working with David Crafoord of Ergonomidesign took this principle one step further. They angled the handle of the **Knife Series 356+** upward by ninety degrees. Users grasp the knife with their entire hand — making a real fist around the handle. Even persons suffering from arthritis can grasp the knife and cut bread. "If we want things to remain as they are, things will have to change," wrote Giuseppe Tomasi di Lampedusa. This also applies particularly to design. Stainless steel and lightweight materials such as plastic and elastomer guarantee the product's ergonomic quality, but the non-slip, safe handle is ingenious. Design will have to leave the beaten path more than ever in the future, so as to ensure that more people continue to lead active lives.

Pushing

If it has to be done quickly then it needs to be pushed, pressed, or hit. **Escape doors** have to withstand quite a bit but should never give in. This principle is very familiar in the USA. Just push on a long horizontal bar and the door opens. The Spanish developers of Dhemen Design perfected these familiar characteristics for the Iberian manufacturer Tesa. Robust mechanics together with clear colors create a product with an immediately obvious function: push me.

The Merten **M-Smart Jumbo** takes this matter equally to heart. Your hands are full but a nudge with an elbow, hip, or knee will do. The large switch can take quite a bit and very obviously questions our established "small is beautiful" aesthetic. Instead of a filigree shape with tiny mechanical parts, the switch is a heavy, oversized device for extreme situations: for instance, if there is little time and your hands are full. Yet the switch really questions the significance of size. Is it really just a matter of dimensions? XXL design will disappear if it is applied in the wrong context. Marketing might like its unique feature aspect, but the true success of XXL design will be determined when put into practice: in a hospital or intensive unit. Inasmuch as the large switch marks a threshold in Universal Design, easily recognizable and intuitively operable, it also functions as a warning against all too frivolous enlargements of familiar objects. Because large does not automatically mean easy to use.

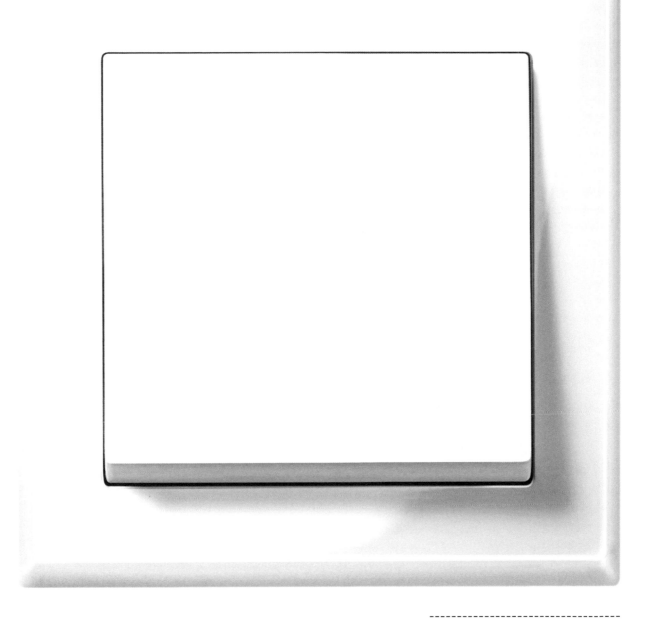

M-Smart Jumbo
Light Switch by Merten,
Size: 160 x 160 mm

XXL design for any use. Turning
the light on with your elbow is
no problem!

Nothing Will Burn Here

The kitchen has once again become the core of the home as the hearth around which everything occurs. It is not simply a matter of eating in the modern kitchen. It also conveys the essence of community and togetherness around the domestic fireplace. A traditional, cozy home notion that Hermann Muthesius in 1917 was still battling when he spoke of "rooms that are technical in nature or concerned with health, such as the bathroom and kitchen, which breathe the familiar spirit of the beautifully designed machine rooms of great factories." He appealed to future designers: "The interior design of our residences will be sleek, unadorned, and practical, after having been flashy and ornate." [49]

[49] Muthesius, Hermann: "Maschinen-arbeit" (Machine work). In: *Technische Abende im Zentralinstitut für Erziehung und Unterricht* (Technical evenings at the Central Institute for Education and Schooling) 4/1917. E. S. Mittler und Sohn, Königliche Hofbuchhandlung. Berlin, 1917, pp. 10—15. *

[50] Lihotzky, Grete: "Rationalization in the Household." In: Anton Kaes, Martin Jay, and Edward Dimendberg (ed.): *The Weimar Republic Sourcebook.* University of California, 1994, pp. 462—5.

Barely a decade later the rational kitchen found its Tayloristic form in 1926 with Grete Lihotzky's Frankfurt kitchen and her statements on "rationalization in the household". [50] Lihotzky wanted to prove that "that simplicity and efficiency are not merely labor-saving but, executed with good materials and the correct form and color, represent clarity and beauty as well."

What has remained besides the standardized built-in kitchens and dimensions? A vision: the idea of the best possible standard of living in the smallest possible environment, the idea of converting the efficiency of machines into day-to-day family life in that the cooking and enjoyment are assigned to what was once the only warm place in the apartment. However, the large family no longer exists and apartments are now well heated. Yet what has remained is the desire to spend pleasant hours together with friends and family. Today's kitchen, as various cooking programs and talk shows make apparent, is now a place to escape work: it has become a place to unwind, and to be free from the sweaty workplace. In this respect it is high time for a new definition of the kitchen if we want to continue seeing it as the warm heart of the home and as a center for togetherness well into age.

If the workspace has also increased in the new forms of the traditional kitchen, then a user's possible restricted mobility is the last thing developers have in mind. Diana Kraus examined this aspect, despite the fact that her project was never about exploring senior-friendly concepts,

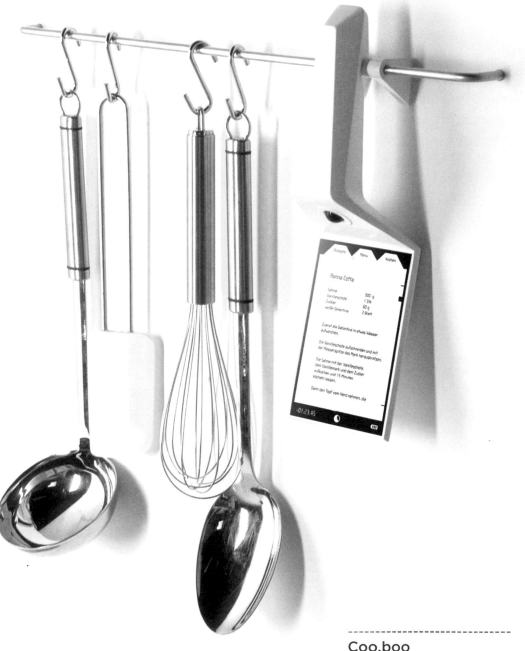

Coo.boo
Digital Cook Book by
Philipp Gilgen

Information right where the
cook needs it. At eye level.

50 plus
Kitchen Concept by Diana Kraus

The kitchen responds to the user's possible restricted movement: equipment is stored within reach; corners are rounded, there are tilted chutes, and much more.

but about following a Universal Design approach that is independent of age or target group. "A kitchen for seniors has to adapt," says the designer. It should compensate for the body and mind's diminishing capabilities, yet actively support the act of cooking. "Safety and ease of orientation can help overcome fear and inhibition. It is imperative to address the target group's core needs for comfort and convenience in the best way possible." An impressive aspiration. But what does it really mean today, in the former machine room of Modernism and in the potential spas of the twenty-first century? The designer first marked out an optimal zone for the most important kitchen work, an area between 40 and 160 centimeters in height. This is allocated for storage and functional elements. That means no low zones or tall cupboards and, hence, no arduous bending or lifting. The work areas are placed so as to be easy on the user's physiology and have been ergonomically optimized. The L- or the U-shaped ground plan is best for preparing, cooking, and washing up in the adjacent corner. "This means an uninterrupted work flow because you can turn from one position to another," says the designer, establishing herself thoroughly within the tradition of Modernism — and realizing the requirements of barrier-free design. A kitchen world of convenience and logical design that goes beyond pure functionalism is a step forward. [51]

51 Particularly as Diana Kraus makes it clear that her design can only "marginally improve the concept of the Frankfurt Kitchen." She wanted to go beyond the laboratory character and its shiny floors, insufficient lighting, strict functionalism, and "scenic Puritanism," even though she also acknowledges that it does connect the "idea of less work time, especially less cooking effort, the aspect of hygiene, and conditions that are set by Küche 50 plus."

The **modular kitchen**, which can be made to adapt to different spatial specifications, offers many possibilities. Its most important parts are movable and make work easier. Hatch doors and movable fixtures are easy on the limbs. Take the sink for instance. Water can be brought to the pot with a fixture that can be extended horizontally. A tilting device on pots and pans helps the cook to drain them.

Designs should not attract attention with extravagant gadgets, but should convince by the sum of good details, which is why Kraus examines a series of innovations in relation to conventional spatial structure. The front edges of countertops curve slightly upward in sensitive areas. They act as both a grab handle and an anti-fall guard for pots and pans. The spice rack is at chest level and can be easily reached; the same applies to the knife block. Crowded storage spaces are replaced by containers for dry goods and fluids. This

Thought through down to every detail: every work area is accessible; standing aids, color-coded water, and electronic support while cooking.

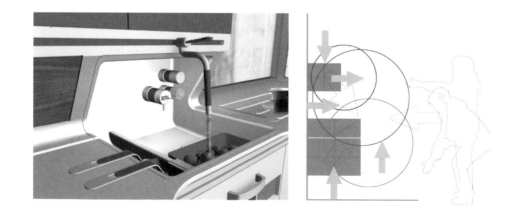

124

is also an indirect reference to the optimized kitchen by Grete Lihotzky, who had already been working with drawers and diverse inserts, although purely from the aspect of efficiency. Since then there has been a clear shift towards more safety and convenience while cooking, which is increasingly considered an enjoyable part of a healthy society. Cooking is "in" and not only on TV.

Diana Kraus designs for everyone. In addition to diverse practical assistance there will be diverse high-tech elements that will enter, if not conquer, the upscale kitchen market in the next few years. Sensors not just for seniors — there will be Internet and communication facilities throughout the entire residence. The computer will cook as well, and not only by means of preset cooking times and recipe suggestions. It will be a virtual chef named Luc, programmed to supply a constant stream of "instructions and tips." The future kitchen responds to touch. When the cook touches a handle, the opaque glass fronts of drawers or refrigerators become transparent thanks to liquid crystal technology. The color-coding of water follows the same principle. A blue or red LED warns against hot water that can burn.

We have discussed the issues of ergonomics and the optimal performance of appliances and technology. But what about aesthetics? The designer wants to embody "simplicity," meaning "decidedly minimal, where the design avoids extravagance." The result — warm wooden veneer combined with metal and curved forms — shows the transformation from a thoroughly rationalized kitchen to one that is part of a domestic space which includes cooking.

52 Lihotzky, Grete: "Rationalization in the Household." In: Anton Kaes, Martin Jay, and Edward Dimendberg (ed.): *The Weimar Republic Sourcebook*. University of California, 1994, pp. 462—5.

53 Degenhart, Christine: *Freiraum. Das Haus fürs Leben, frei von Barrieren*. Landkreis Rosenheim (ed.), 2000.

Yet of course innovations do not emerge out of the blue. The Miele company was involved in developing the model. As Grete Lihotzky once said, "The problem of rationalizing the household, therefore, cannot be solved in isolation, but must go hand-in-hand with associated social considerations." [52] The fact that future kitchen concepts would play a key role in designing apartments and other living spaces was apparently not yet known. Autonomy in older age means wide-ranging self-sufficiency, according to architect Christine Degenhart of the Barrier-free Building Information Center at the Bavarian Chamber of Architecture. [53] The task for future design is to maintain and support this degree of freedom.

FOOT

Superplan XXL
Shower Basin by Phoenix Design

Comfortable to enter and equipped with anti-slip enameling.

A DESIGNER HAS TO REACH A CERTAIN AGE BEFORE HE OR SHE CAN IMAGINE WHAT IT'S LIKE TO BE OLD.

MARTIN HAUENSTEIN

Foot

Mobility begins in the mind. But what to do with a society that is chained to a computer and turns tennis arms and slipped disks into a popular sport? Even sophisticated technology cannot compensate for lack of movement, but it could, however, offer some relief. If you have to sit down for the entire day, manufacturers of diverse office furniture say to do it in an active manner. But those who cannot move at all are dependant on outside assistance and, since relatives help less and less in this regard, there may well come a day when the Personal Service Robot serves breakfast in bed.

We sit too much. Physiotherapists have been telling us for ages to get up from the desk more often and stretch our tired joints, muscles, and tendons. But someone who is truly chained to the keyboard can now rely on the **Stitz**, the classic by Hans (Nick) Roericht. Even the name elegantly conveys the idea of standing and sitting. The single-leg leaning aid stands on a base filled with quartz sand and supports the user's weight, while he or she leans on a stand-up desk. The height of the Stitz can be controlled by a lever under the seat on the telescope bar. The Stitz, which has been awarded many prizes, provides the additional height in cases where normal chairs fall too short: between counter height and table, drawing board and computer workplace. It supports but does not carry its user. He or she has to stand alone. The Stitz encourages its user to get up and start moving naturally again.

Doors Suddenly Open

Comfort is the main gateway for Universal Design, as well as simple operation and general manageability. And this is felt where one least expects it: within one's own four walls. **Porteo** can open doors as heavy as 80 kilos without its 6-centimeter installation height being too significant. Porteo can be operated by a hand-held remote control and has been awarded the iF Hanover "Universal Design Award" because it marries technology with aesthetics, foregoes long cables, and is simple to install — meaning it also makes rooms accessible that previously presented a challenge. Universal Design is more than anti-slip floor coverings and barrier-free bathrooms, more than optional aids and handles in the necessary places. Universal Design weaves throughout our day-to-day life, from head to feet.

Adiplus
Ergonomic Runnig Shoe by
Stephanie Hudde

The biomechanically cushioned inserted
sole and ergonomic pull tabs on the
instep and tongue are unique features of
this running shoe.

Walk Well

Design's reputation as a mere shell changed a long time ago. Design boosts engineering knowledge with new possibilities, or searches for innovative, simple, and pragmatic solutions that make life easier. Anyone who has ever had to limp away from a sports field knows the importance of mobility. We all want to be able to walk with ease, and technology can help. Technological aids for running athletes are growing rapidly. Gel insoles, shock absorbers, and elastic materials now belong to the standard equipment of even half-hearted hobby runners. No wonder that the **Adiplus running shoe** was developed for the 50-plus group.

Stephanie Hudde of FH Coburg has demonstrated how aesthetics and function, safety and comfort, can all be integrated into a running shoe. Firstly, the familiar sole can still be used. On the outside, the shoe looks like a normal shoe. The differences and nuances are on the inside; a "biomechanical spring cushion" provides the user with excellent foothold on streets, sidewalks, and forest paths. Secondly, safety and comfort are not just labels attached to the outside of the shoe; they have worked their way into the details. Reflectors increase safety at night and straps attached to the insteps and tongue make the shoe easy to put on and take off. It seems that Adiplus has put an end to fumbling with laces and tongues.

Whoever is not very mobile (at the moment) can look to the **Toyota iReal**, which *Stern* magazine dubbed a "mobile electronic vehicle." The slender, one-seat vehicle breaks the tradition of previous car, moped, and bicycle mobility concepts and brings the speedy wheelchair to mind. The high-tech, inner-city vehicle helps us right where and when we need it most: shopping. It whizzes around a mall at 40 kilometers an hour from store to store, demonstrating how a large car company such as Toyota can become an all-round mobility corporation. According to the Japanese, PM — Personal Mobility — is the future. A series of swift, helpful means of transportation that can serve to assist a society that is gradually becoming older and frailer, but also anyone who needs help at the moment. The first steps have been made toward Universal Design in the field of mobility. And we will all profit from it.

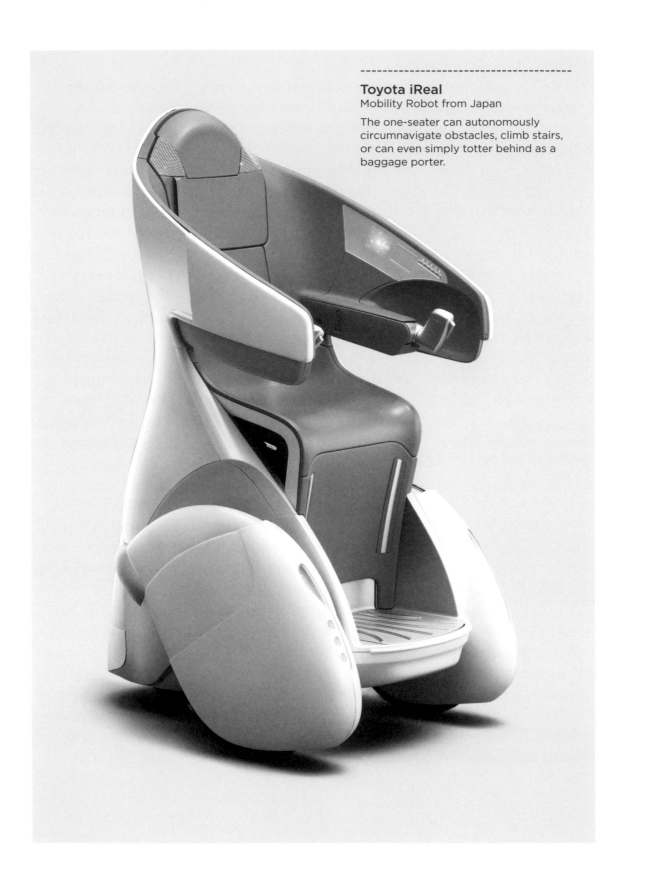

Toyota iReal
Mobility Robot from Japan

The one-seater can autonomously circumnavigate obstacles, climb stairs, or can even simply totter behind as a baggage porter.

Mobility Despite Age

Mobility is not a just a question of infrastructure or a preferred means of transportation. It is indicative of a flexible mind, and is no longer directly related to physical fitness. A healthy mind can exist in a not very healthy body, or vice versa.

54 *Vierter Altenbericht zur Lage der älteren Generation in der Bundesrepublik Deutschland* (The fourth age report on the condition of older generations in Federal Republic of German): *Risiken, Lebensqualität und Versorgung Hochaltriger — unter besonderer Berücksichtigung Erkrankungen* (Risks: quality of life and the care of the elderly — with special attention given to dementia diseases), 2004, p. 77. *

55 Ibid., p. 218. Inflexible, insufficient public local transportation is criticized in particular, "Whoever has no car, or no longer has a car is dependant on public transportation. But this almost no longer exists. It is difficult even now in some towns to get from A to B and back again in the same day." Translated from: Schweitzer, Hanne: *Kommentar zum 5. Altenbericht der Bundesregierung.* Büro gegen Altersdiskriminierung e. V., 10.3.2006 ("Commentary on the fifth age report by the federal office against age discrimination"); http://www.altersdiskriminierung.de/themen/artikel.php?id=1576.

Technology can help with physical limitations because new forms of communication are becoming more important — such as the Internet that not only eases the task of providing for day-to-day needs, but also helps with networking, or staying in contact with friends and family. Today, our level of mobility determines whether we remain integrated within the social network, and how we are viewed and accepted by others. The 2004 fourth age report on the condition of the older generation formulated this as follows: "Whereas the term mobility for middle-aged adults or the 'young-old' generation refers to transportation, particularly one's own car, mobility for the elderly often refers to the day-to-day ability to move, walk, and climb stairs. Activities that were once taken for granted become an effort in old age." [54] For this reason, a means of transportation remains vital to a fulfilled, natural, and accepted life. People no longer mobile are quickly left behind, and society communicates this well. Which is why experts say that, "driving a car for older people is often key to their sense of self-worth," adding however that, "far more significant is the fact that the car is a resource that is very difficult to forfeit, when growing older and becoming less mobile, if a person wants to remain mobile and lead a natural life, nor can it be replaced by other technical and environmental resources (public local transport)." [55]

All On Board!

The trend of wanting to own a car remains unbroken. Half of all German new cars are purchased by the fifty-plus generation, and they also purchase 80 percent of luxury class cars. [56] But where are the multigeneration automobile ideas? Those which are easy to enter and have user-friendly displays? What use is the most beautiful car in the world if no one can use it? The mixture of an intact brand image, good design, and an intact, healthy back can be found in the Porsche Cayenne, whose wide doors, raised entry level, and elevated driving position have earned it the dubious reputation of being a senior-Porsche. [57] Both marketing and corporate communications are speechless when luxury manufacturers are asked about the car. This can only mean that, in addition to safety [58] and ecology, comfort and convenience will be the main focus for designers and car manufacturers in the future. As usual, suggestions often come out of the universities, as Martin Könecke has shown in his degree dissertation: Elegant lines, reduced cockpit, white interior. The design study would do honor to any limousine, yet it does not stop at the surface. Suddenly the driver's seat swings to the side and upwards. Exactly 180 millimeters upward and 30 degrees toward the direction of traffic. This is made possible by a unique mounted suspension on the central console and leg area. Martin Könecke designed a unique **mounting system for car seats** for his degree dissertation. [59] It adapts to fit drivers so they can enter and exit the vehicle more easily. Ergonomics at its most beautiful and, because the seat is mounted only on one side, more space inside the car.

56 Scheytt, Stefan: "Woopies. Sie haben Geld. Sie haben Zeit. Und alte Menschen können noch eine Menge brauchen." *brand eins* 9/2005.

57 "For that to remain so unquestionable, the car industry has to adapt its products to our needs. That means that seats can't be positioned virtually at ground level, but should be friendly to our old bones. The Cayenne, or the senior-Porsche, with its wide doors and high seats, is a model product. It communicates that electronic parking aids, an easy to understand navigation system, and an easy to use radio device are natural features of any automobile." Von Kuehnheim, Haug: "Gib Gas, Alter!" In: *Die Zeit* No. 11, March 9, 2006. *

58 "For over 75-years-old, after falls, car accidents are the second most common cause of injury and the most common cause of fatal injuries [...]. The rate of recurrence of car accidents among Alzheimer sufferers is comparable to the under 26-year-old group, but double that of drivers with no physical restrictions." *Vierter Altenbericht zur Lage der älteren Generation*, 2004, p. 174. *

59 Martin Könecke's dissertation at the FHH entitled "Senioren Fahrzeuginterieur" (Automobile interiors for seniors) won the first Universal Design competition in Lower Saxony. The work was supervised by Professor Gunnar Spellmeyer and the head of the design department at EDAG Engineering + Design AG in Fulda, Johannes Barckmann.

Senior Car Interior
Design by Martin Könecke

Assists the user while getting in and out of the car. A special mounted system allows the car seat to swing outward and upward.

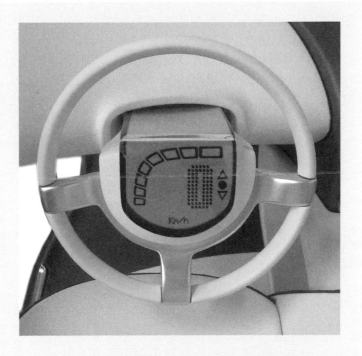

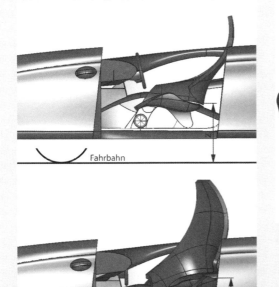

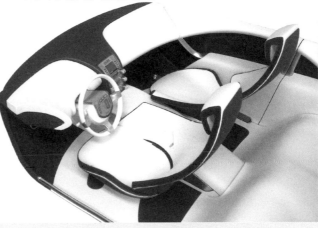

Even if Könecke primarily had older people in mind, he created a design for everyone who wants a more comfortable solution. The prizewinner of the 2007 Universal Design competition in Lower Saxony deliberately chose a light, formal language in order to avoid any association with orthopedics. Because Universal Design has nothing at all to do with stigmatization and is not limited to one target group. What is good for older people is good for everyone.

The Speedy Wheelchair

First you hear a buzzing sound, then a halogen lamp illuminates the forest path and a small vehicle whizzes by. Branches slap against the curved Plexiglas bonnet protecting the driver. Two astonished hikers move to the side of the path. That is not how they imaged the first four-wheel drive, outdoor hybrid wheelchair. The woman behind the joystick says hello and speeds past. The path is rocky and uphill, but the vehicle carries on undisturbed. The seat has an automatic tilt feature, meaning electronics compensate for extreme inclines. The driver can operate the joystick intuitively and directly by hand. The two hikers smile at each other after

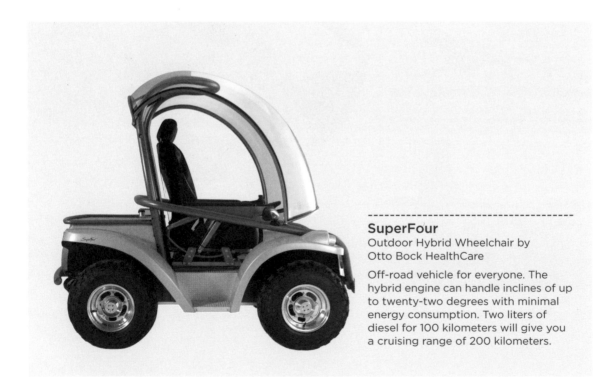

SuperFour
Outdoor Hybrid Wheelchair by
Otto Bock HealthCare

Off-road vehicle for everyone. The hybrid engine can handle inclines of up to twenty-two degrees with minimal energy consumption. Two liters of diesel for 100 kilometers will give you a cruising range of 200 kilometers.

the dust has settled. I'd like one of those, says one of the hikers. The other does not reply, she wipes the sweat from her brow and continues up the hill.

Otto Bock HealthCare, the manufacturer of orthopedic and rehabilitation products aims to mass produce, rather than custom make, the **Superfour outdoor wheelchair**. The company now wants to enter new markets, rather than serve the needs of a small but discriminating target group. Swiss designer Urs Schoenauer is responsible for the speedy fun wheelchair — an off-road vehicle that can handle an incline of up to twenty-two degrees or about forty percent from ground level. The hybrid engine has a stationary generator, four hub motors, and a differential electronic system that distributes force as needed, depending on terrain, to four wheels, which makes the vehicle extremely agile. And because the wheelchair is devised for "active wheelchair users" who appreciate being self-sufficient and mobile, the independent wheel suspension is equipped with 100-millimeter spring deflection, making the SuperFour a comfortable and all-terrain vehicle.

The TAS (Tourist assistance system for barrier-free access) navigation system combined with a mobile radio link means additional safety and constant communication. In the future, this will be further developed into a comprehensive information system, answering questions such as: Where is the nearest drug store? Or the most interesting museum? Doesn't an old friend live somewhere around here? The vehicle has a cruising range of 200 kilometers on two liters of diesel fuel per 100 kilometers. The car has always been a symbol of autarchy and safety, and now this compact vehicle offers those benefits to all user groups. A push of a button and the seat pivots to the front axle for easy entry. Enter the vehicle, close the Plexiglas bonnet and drive off. If a direction is developing in mobile Universal Design then it is: walking stick > rollator > outdoor mobility. In other words from rehabilitation products to design for all.

Peter Naumann, Professor of Industrial Design at the
University of Applied Sciences in Munich, on new automotive
concepts, chic auto interiors, and helpful assistants

OH **Our society is as mobile as ever. More and more cars entering the
market are geared to increasingly specified target groups. How
do car manufacturers perceive older people?**

PN With ambivalence. No one has considered the over-seventy target
group, and it took published studies to make them realize that
this is a rather solvent target group, interested in premium products. They are fulfilling a dream and want to be young and active.
This target group, however, does not necessarily say that's a
Golf Plus, the right car for our age group, and we'll buy it for this
reason.

OH **So it is about soft factors, about the right image.**

PN That is surely one reason for the success of the SUV (sport utility
vehicle) that provides a high level of comfort when entering the
car. This concept is very well packaged. A car that looked like
a truck or van would be uninteresting, because it is not stylish.
The after work, dream-come-true moment is important, which
is particularly relevant for manufacturers such as Porsche. Many
cars are purchased, not because customers can afford them, but
they are able to afford them.

OH **Able to afford them?**

PN That means not needing the money for something more essential.
This target group is now recognized and important because they
will have the money to buy premier cars, as well as other things.

OH **On the other hand, this is dispraised as the "Porsche for the
elderly" because the driver can enter the car more easily.**

PN The car's success was at first surprising; its advantages need to be better communicated in the future, because they are comfortable and family-friendly. A family would not really buy a Porsche Cayenne, but maybe a grandparent would, so he or she could do something together with the children and grandchildren. It has a lot of luggage space. At the moment the trend is leaning toward more functionality. I want to be able to do more with my car.

OH **That doesn't fully explain the success of this car.**

PN Psychology plays a role. They embody safety and good protection for both passengers and the environment. You sit higher and move within a small fortress.

OH **Cars are becoming do-it-alls, they are now more accessible for older people and at the same time more stylish. They embody safety and offer comfort; are we heading toward a type of racy living-room car for city use?**

PN Precisely. The car should become a part of life. The comfort idea marks the emancipation from technical overkill. If anything, customers say that high-tech is great but we would rather not see it and do not want it to be too complex to operate. Anything but monitors everywhere and thousands of buttons. On the other hand, certain archaic operational elements should remain. We'd like to continue turning a knob to raise or lower the volume, and not to get lost in menus and decision trees. This applies to many things from MP3 players to video recorders. In today's day and age, the product doesn't have to broadcast its capabilities. Technology can take a back seat. In contrast, things that we think are particularly wonderful or beautiful, such as food and furniture, can come to the fore.

OH **What does that mean in terms of a mobile life?**

PN That you can get in, feel comfortable, and not doubt your ability to operate everything. Ambience plays a big role. I am being driven; the car is taking over more and more responsibility so that driving is fun again. A nice side effect. Driving becomes more defensive. Something older people appreciate. Car manufacturers should think about what their product projects. Should it be used aggressively? Stylish and sporty, yes, but please tone it down.

OH	**How would you design a stylish car for the over-seventy group?**
PN	It should not look senior-friendly at all. Drivers do not want to be branded as being old, even if they are no longer as agile as they once were. The changes to the cars need to be more far-reaching.
OH	**What must tangibly change?**
PN	It starts with getting into the car. This aspect has not yet been considered from the perspective of the drivers, but is rather only designed to support the stability of the car. As soon as you lay a hand on this feature, you have to develop a completely new car. Then loading and unloading the car. In the future it should be possible to do this without getting whiplash from reaching too high or bending too low. Storage areas of cars should function like a conveyor belt, they should move towards the drivers or lower away from them. The handle to release the luggage com-partment door has already been moved inside the car to make it easier to operate; this could be done electrically in the future. The seats are also a major issue, especially ventilation in summer. We also have to get a grip on the drivers' workplaces. Another important topic is automotive safety technologies, such as Pre-crash systems that automatically provide brake support in order to avoid a collision. Or communication between vehicles to warn them about accidents ahead.
OH	**A talking car?**
PN	Speech systems are a huge topic, not a cure-all, but a new science with enormous potential. You can do a lot with speech. The system asks, "Which district do you want to drive to?" And the driver answers, "the center" or says "one," which stands for the center of town. The emphasis is on command, on and off, and figures.
OH	**What are the limits of automotive safety technologies?**
PN	They are not clear. Automotive safety technologies address you personally, they are very persuasive. They help you identify things and they also observe the driver; they sense if the driver momen-tarily drops off or becomes aggressive. The system could even change color to inform others on the road that this driver is angry.

OH   **These are completely new perspectives. The driver will be observed and the on-board computer takes control in dangerous situations. Until now, you sat behind the wheel and thought you were the driver. Will that be a problem?**

PN   The driver will always be the active driver. But he or she can also decide if they want assistance. If so, the car can take over and enter the road traffic using GPS and sensors. It will increasingly be able to do things alone, even taking over in certain situations. For instance, getting on the highway, something that is particularly difficult for older people. The ability to judge distance and speed diminishes with age and this is where the car can help.

OH   **So it will still be about choice and not force.**

PN   No one will accept Big Brother. I can do a lot myself but automatic systems help a great deal.

OH   **It will become easier, more comfortable, and safer with redundant systems, speech recognition, and buttons. What will it feel like to drive in the future?**

PN   As you want it to feel. The driver concentrates on the street and no longer has to deal with unnecessary things or get lost in menus. Ergonomists say that humans are only able to manage three levels at any given time. Driving is of course the first level. Any other activity can therefore only involve two levels. On the other hand, many things aren't used because they are hidden. There has to be a great rethinking. Otherwise you could introduce the wrong product to the market.

OH   **Therefore, the interior will become as essential as the exterior ...**

PN   ... exactly. And the ambient perhaps even more so. The exterior needs to be elegant, stylish, but the interior will be — as in architecture — an experience. Individualization is the magic word, from special wood inlays to user interfaces. With options for display graphics, speech, and sounds. It should be fun and give customers the feeling that they own a very unique car.

OH   **For older people, these interfaces would have larger, easy-to-read menus. They are the most hard-to-please customers, the most experienced; they place value on workmanship, on aesthetics, and functions. They will set the standards in the future and will be more demanding.**

PN   Absolutely. Manufacturers have to start rethinking, away from technological bombast, away from the niche product. If older people can enjoy things, it means that others can also benefit from the additional comfort. It is essential that no one be discriminated against. Demographic development is in any case a wonderful reason to rethink our products in a reasonable manner, so that they can benefit everyone.

How Should We Design a Home?

It will soon be impossible to dismiss one of the oldest questions in human history with the dualistic "residing — living" sales-promotion jargon. The house or apartment is the only commodity other than the car that so intensely reflects the desires and beliefs of entire generations. But the old motto, "Show me how you live and I'll tell you who you are" is only partly true for the fifty-plus generation. Layouts and furnishings will no longer necessarily reflect desire, but rather the prospect of economic potential paired with the knowledge that physical fitness will most likely decrease.

First the numbers: residential space will increase and continue to increase. The expansion of residential zones is a phenomenon in any industrial state. In 2003 the Danes and Luxemburgers had an average of fifty square meters of residential space; two years earlier the Americans had over sixty-two square meters. The trend toward more space applies to all age groups. For Germany, a study by empirica Communication and Technology Research forecasts an increase of nineteen percent to 4.4 billion square meters of residential space between 2005 and 2030, despite a diminishing population figure. [60] To reach this figure, 330,000 residential units will have to be created each year.

60 Braun, Reiner; Pfeiffer, Ulrich: *Wohnflächennachfrage in Deutschland* (Living space requirements in Germany). Empirica, Berlin, 2005.

Another interesting question: older people need more living space per head. The space available to them "clearly increases with age despite the fact that the size of apartments (residential space per household) is stagnating or even decreasing. The most significant reason for this is that households typically remain in the family home (residual effect) even after the children have left or a spouse has deceased." [61]

61 Braun, Reiner; Pfeiffer, Ulrich: *Wohnflächennachfrage in Deutschland.* Empirica, Berlin, 2005, p. 4.

62 Krings-Heckemeier, Marie-Therese: *Das silberne Zeitalter — Wie wir den Wandel zu einer Gesellschaft der erweiterten Lebensspannen bewältigen können.* Empirica, Berlin, 2007.

63 According to an Empirica study, this figure of fifty percent for the over fifty-year-olds is higher that the national average of forty-seven percent. In southern Germany, the percentage of owners is even higher.

The size of the home as a rule grows until the age of fifty. The increase in square meters directly reflects an increase in the level of wealth, which all generations continue to drive upward. And there are related studies and attempts at classification here as well. One study by empirica commissioned by the Federal State Home Loan Bank speculates that two thirds of the 31 million people in the fifty-plus generation "consider changing their home situation or have already done so," and that this trend is growing. [62] Now, perhaps not much can be expected from a study commissioned by a bank, yet the overwhelming percentage of household mobility that emerges here is illuminating nonetheless. Yet, whether it is a matter of so-called asset optimizers — mainly property owners — or those choosing to move and looking for a "smaller house or an apartment in a central location with an elevator," the one main priority is to "remain independent for as long as possible and in close proximity to family and friends." A surprising consequence of negative population development and a preexisting high rate of home ownership [63] is that although the country's population is decreasing, the number of households is increasing. This is mainly due to the rise in households of older people. Renovating, building extensions, upgrading, and modernizing will be the focus of tomorrow. Taking Regensburg as an example will illustrate the difficulties of renovating and rebuilding protected historic buildings. But what about new buildings? With aesthetics and innovations? The following examples from Austria and Switzerland communicate a desire to build as well as show that buildings are not merely dwellings; they can also provide design-added value without neglecting standards and amenities. Innovation and aesthetics form the basis for a new architecture for all generations.

Barrier-free Building as the Task of the Future

The 2004 fourth age report, which analyzes the condition of the older generation, unmistakably shows that "in addition to financial control, maintaining an independent life and successfully managing day-to-day affairs is of utmost importance to older people — which also goes hand in hand with their financial resources. This is where the home and the home environment can form the essential base of independence, contentment, and ultimately quality of life in old age." [64]

[64] *Vierter Altenbericht zur Lage der älteren Generation*, 2004, p. 106. *

The findings, however, vary greatly. Aesthetics often play a rather insignificant role when people are the focus. And again, buildings cannot compensate for a lack of social contact, yet to pit ethics against a lack of aesthetics and to dismiss the supposed added expense of a designer as wasted money will be more difficult in the future, after good examples have shown what can effectively be achieved. Rebuilding society as well as its already existing shell, the houses and cities, will take place gradually. And we often get caught in the perfection trap — everything has to be 100 percent, DIN standards, and first-class. Yet maybe we will not be able to afford this luxury in the future, and will be happy as long as converted structures provide sixty percent more for their residents, even if critics object to the missing forty percent. It is a matter of the art of modesty, also the art of achieving more with less. The ramp at the entrance is often merely a symbol; it is far more essential to design open spaces so that they can be used more flexibly. It is a matter of using local resources and often simply to improvise.

AGE IS NOT AN ILLNESS.

DIANA KRAUS

Christine Degenhart, spokesperson for the Barrier-free Building
Information Center of the Bavarian Chamber of Architecture, on
standards and laws

OH   **Where are we in relation to a senior-friendly society that should eventually be reflected in legislation?**

CD   With regard to products that have a sustained influence on people, and I include buildings here, the situation looks rather good in Germany. This has to do with anti-discrimination laws and state building regulations. Legislators are already acting, but the market is only now waking up to the issue.

OH   **Why isn't the market reacting?**

CD   Because their products reflect demand and thus society. The market moves slowly and the many small initiatives do matter, such as residential communities for Alzheimer's patients and the senile or residential communities for older women. These are individual examples that can start things going …

OH   **… but on an interpersonal level, without standards.**

CD   We do want to develop standards, and this is where planners are really needed. The most important thing is that we can achieve a goal using different means. Legislators have approached the matter clear-sightedly, and many communities have already become aware of the resources they owe their citizens, so they can age with dignity and care. These advancements stimulate the market.

OH   **It is very different for one-family homes; I see no barrier-free living there.**

CD   People are free to choose and it is left to their own initiative. But individual responsibility is also very important because legislators are not planning to pass barrier-free ordinances for private homes. Barrier-free accessibility has to be demanded, even by the property developers, since supply reacts to demand. Architecture and ground plans will change as soon as the population begins to demand barrier-free buildings. Even the cost of, for instance, installing showers flush with the floor level will come down. Nonetheless, here and in the transition zones between balconies and terraces there is a looming risk of liability in terms of building physics.

OH **And a conflict of norms.**

CD That too. The industry is needed here as well as the standards committee. This is also where pressure from the market will bring about the relevant changes.

OH **Barrier-free accessibility is a very popular subject. How many norms and laws exist, and how are they graded?**

CD Dozens. Building regulations are responsible for policies concerning residential units and the design of public access areas. There are also agreements under private law, similar to DIN standards, as well as compulsory standards set by state building regulations. Compulsory ordinances apply nationally. In restaurants for example, it is now mandatory to have handicapped-access, and therefore senior-friendly toilets.

OH **DIN standards relate only to Germany and are not transferable.**

CD Possibly they are. It always depends on who takes the initiative and captures national interest at the standards committee. If a norm exists, it is much easier to act from the state's perspective. Moreover, from a European point of view, existing legislation can play a role.

Where Are We Now?

OH **Where are we in comparison with Europe as a whole?**

CD Germany was once a leader in barrier-free building norms and many of these were adopted by other German-speaking countries. But this situation has reversed and today Germany does not play a leading role in developing EU norms. Other countries are dealing with the issue much more pragmatically from the onset …

OH   **... for example?**

CD   Sweden. Their attitude is that public access toilets should be available for both women and men alike. They are also completely barrier-free and hence senior-friendly. As Sweden shows us here, a social consensus can do more than just generate norms.

OH   **In which direction is legislation heading?**

CD   Simplification is an important goal to follow in general. The EU wants to reduce the number of laws and to merge related issues, so that each and every knob or handle does not have to be described individually. There should be one general description for knobs and handles that people can operate or use at a certain height. Cost will also be considered. But there should be clear key data to provide a framework within which designers can move about freely.

OH   **How do architects deal with norms? Do they see them as restricting or as a motivating challenge?**

CD   Every restriction has a liberating aspect and also leads to new ideas. Setbacks (the distance between buildings) and firewalls are supposed to protect people. They present a challenge to every planner. How do I place a firewall? Should I orchestrate it? Barrier-free accessibility means, however, that people's safety in terms of the law is not directly affected. There is noticeably less pressure and suddenly the creative energy derived from the restriction begins to flag. For some architects, restrictions such as these are a yoke, for others, an interesting challenge.

OH   **In general: can the challenge of aging be solved by norms?**

CD   With great limitations, yes. There are things that simply have to function. Barrier-free access is not debatable. The building can be beautifully designed, but if I can't get in, it doesn't function. Everything else should be free to change with time, fashion, habits, and the occupants' shifting level of fitness. DIN norms are not always beneficial here, but the most important narrow passages, for instance in the bathroom where autonomy is desired, should be defined and documented with figures and geometry. The resulting key data will allow for a well-designed bathroom.

Integrated Housing
Restoration work on listed property belonging to the Stadtbau Regensburg GmbH

A glass elevator connects two buildings of an historic complex. Thirty-three disabled-friendly and barrier-free apartments were created in the grounds of a former brewery. The exemplary project won the Deutsche Städtebaupreis (German urban planning prize) in 2000.

Converting Asserts — Integrated Housing in Regensburg

The future belongs to renovations or conversions, whether in the suburbs or the city, in relatively modern buildings, or in the historical center of town. Because one thing is certain: new buildings will be erected less and less, as we will need to convert the existing structure of our cities to match shifts in demography. Yet this involves a preprogrammed conflict. The norms and standards that applied to areas that were previously unrelated will begin to overlap or even collide: for instance the protection of historical buildings and the need to convert them into barrier-free buildings. How this conflict of objectives might be solved can only be established on site. Regensburg, a city on the Danube, demonstrates both future developments and rejections in one concentrated area: World Cultural Heritage and growth center in one, a high-tech location and an historical address. Important buildings are packed densely together in the old town; district after district is being renovated and modernized to meet today's standards. Yet the standards are getting higher and always changing. And what about senior-friendly renovations? An epitome of conversion was created as early as 1995 on the outskirts of the historical center, on a quiet side street leading to the Danube. A former brewery was converted into thirty-three handicapped-accessible and barrier-free apartments of various sizes, ranging from one and a half room apartments to four room apartments, plus community and social facilities. [65] It was possible to implement a flexible concept, which in larger apartments included either a children's bedroom or a therapy room, because the architects and building owners were one and the same. Klaus Nickelkoppe of Stadtbau Regensburg GmbH assumed the task of constructing a completely barrier-free development in the heart of the city at the lowest possible cost.

The integrated residential development was awarded the Deutsche Städtebaupreis (German urban development prize) in 2000. From the air it looks like a massive H. Bridges from a glass elevator in a green

[65] In developers terms this means a barrier-free renovation of a historically protected complex with wheelchair access to the city. Every apartment is barrier-free, of which fifteen units conform to DIN 18025 part 1 and 18 WE to DIN 18025 part 2. See *Barrierefreies und Integriertes Wohnen. Forschungsbericht zur Nachuntersuchung ausgewählter Projekte aus Modellvorhaben und Landeswettbewerb* (Barrier-free and integrated homes. Research reports on the follow-up of selected projects from model plans and national competition). Oberste Baubehörde im Bayerischen Staatsministerium des Inneren (Supreme building authority of the Bavarian State Ministry of the Interior) (ed.): Materialien zum Wohnungsbau. Munich, 2006.

courtyard connect the two buildings that face out to different streets. The addition functions as a hub for the entire complex and relieves the strain on the historical ensemble whose supporting structure and window axis needed to be preserved; dividing walls could be easily shifted within the complex and were modernized to fulfill today's requirements. Special prefabricated bathroom furnishings made of melamine formaldehyde resin were added. Protecting historical buildings can in fact be converted into barrier-free structures — given the right basic conditions.

There is a green courtyard between the buildings. The heart of the complex in the middle of the densely built old city is an oasis for residents, who meet on the footbridges between the two buildings halves. There are communal balconies here with benches and plants that create a meeting area that has an almost southern European feeling. A research group at the Technical University in Munich established that "only a few residents reported a desire to become acquainted with their neighbors. Life here is similar to a normal apartment complex." That is perhaps the greatest compliment for the developers: normality in a residential building for everyone, the old and the young, for people without or without disabilities. A residential building that is open to the changes in our society and that includes its residents in the network of the city, with Arnulfplatz directly outside their front door.

Comfortable and Active: Adult Care Facility in Domat/Ems by Dietrich Schwarz

This model offers the potential of both an independent life in one's own apartment and available support, if necessary. A residential concept that unites the amenities of both an apartment and a care facility, that is, quietude and care, contact with others, a view of the landscape, and high-quality amenities. The adult care facility in Domat/Ems is a barrier-free environment. It is an extension of the existing old age home and offers twenty, fifty-two square meter large two-room apartments on four stories. The distribution of the units that pierce through or are reflected in the ground plan as pairs is as simple as it is functional: the living room and terrace comprise one half of the apartment; the other half, protected, contains the kitchen and bedroom looking over the Alps.

The development follows an energy-optimized concept and is built to face south. Its north face is monolithically closed. The building is

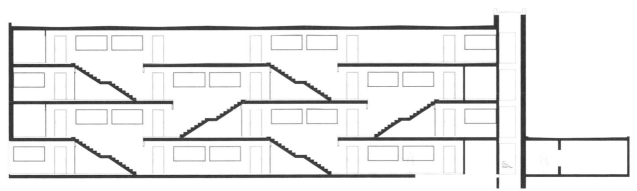

Adult Care Facility
Residential Concept in Domat/Ems
by Dietrich Schwarz

Twenty, one-bedroom apartments, each
fifty-two square meters in size, on four
floors, perfectly accessible. A refuge for
an independent life.

On-grade home interiors and barrier-free bathrooms support an independent life for seniors of any age.

defined by precision and a consistent use of quality materials. The south-facing facade opens generously out to the landscape. A highly efficient construction of glass and metal envelops every level like a shimmering shell; the levels in turn alternate between terraces and large glazed living rooms that have only one point of reference: light and sun. The interiors are bright and spacious, the rooms flow from one into the other, and sliding doors give an even more spacious feel to the apartments. The kitchens and bathrooms are designed to be thoroughly barrier-free, equipped with accessible sinks, wide doorways, and walk-in showers. And the most impressive aspect is that the design does not suffer by any means.

66 See Schwarz, Dietrich: "Sustainable Design". In: *Werkbundsiedlung Wiesenfeld*. Volume 5. (Werkbundtage 2. Material und Technik). Munich, 2007, pp. 89—97.

Architect Dietrich Schwarz plays with contrasts. Parquet and steel, nature and technology, warm and cold. Floor-to-ceiling glazing opens up the interior space to the outdoors, more connected than separated by a threshold, a winter garden with large sliding doors. References to the outside characterize life in the interior. Across from the light-flooded living room and bedroom are the community areas in the stairwell, which are visible through a fireproof window in the kitchen. This stairwell serves as the backbone and spatial continuum of the complex and extends through the entire building. It is an alternative to the wheelchair-accessible elevator and also functions as a visual link. Every apartment has its own storage room on the same floor. There are cellar divisions, which greatly reduce thermal bridges. The entire building is Minergie-P standard certified by the HTA in Lucerne and is energy optimized. The solar collecting facades developed by Büro Dietrich Schwarz and the Swiss Federal Office of Energy become the core design elements of the building and are massive energy collectors. Heating pumps and solar collectors work in unison. A ventilation system provides round-the-clock fresh air to the rooms. The building services are located in three compact rooms on the top floor. Büro Dietrich Schwarz in Zurich set new standards at Domat/Ems for the comfort, aesthetics, and energy balance of a residential complex that also, above all, offers a space for people to develop. Where else can you find another example of this achievement? The adult care facility at Domat/Ems with twenty apartments at the foot of the Tuma Falveng was even awarded a solar prize. The south-facing apartments and their special, energy-saving solar windows [66] with a view to the mountains were awarded the Swiss Solar Prize.

Carlo Baumschlager and Dietmar Eberle from Austria are established names in residential construction. Despite their worldwide projects, the "grands seigneurs" of Vorarlberg building culture have a predilection for good residential construction. Initially the St. Gallen Achslengut Residences (second phase of construction) reveal nothing at all, nor do the Eichgut Residences in Winterthur or the Lohbach Residences, Innsbruck. The barrier-free housing estates are no different to other quality projects by the architect duo: clear spaces, unique shading solutions, central corridors, and spectacular wellholes. So what then makes them so special? Both barrier-free Swiss projects demonstrate a cool elegance reminiscent of Helvetia graphics. The second construction phase of the **Achslengut Residences** in St. Gallen, with its 126 apartments built in 2002, plays with one of Baumschlager Eberle's signature elements: residential towers together with a fluid shell. These barrier-free units offer a view of Lake Constance and each is enveloped by a partly transparent and partly translucent glazed sliding element. The **Eichgut Residences** were completed in 2005 and contain ninety apartments. Here, the shell is modeled into a wonderfully expressive element in the form of a type of scaled armor that seems to cover the elongated building, which flexes with protrusions and recesses, and creates a double facade. This outer shell establishes a balance between the conflicting elements of protection and fragility. Protection because the development is located behind Winterthur's main train station, and fragility because of the complex's rather solid, angular appearance. The double skin of screen-printed glass panels forms an optic and acoustic umbrella against the outer world, if the residents so desire. Barrier-free accessibility was an important criterion during the construction phase. The elevator leads directly to the apartment, which means convenience and access. The residential units are lit by daylight from the street and the inner courtyard. They range from 88 to 155 square meters in size, with some extending from one side of the building to the other at as much as twenty-seven meters in depth. They have been designed as a flowing spatial volume in which bathroom units and other furnishings float like islands in an open sea of living space. The apartments have been awarded a Swiss Minergie-Standard-P certificate and are energy optimized, boasting an annual energy consumption of only nine-kilowatt

Achslengut
Residences in St. Gallen by
Baumschlager Eberle

126 barrier-free residential units, concentrated in eight residential towers. With a
view of Lake Constance.

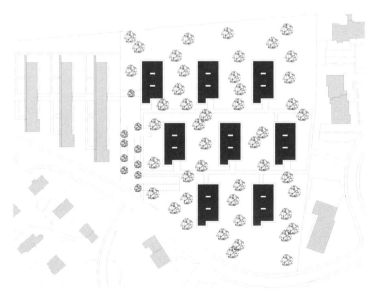

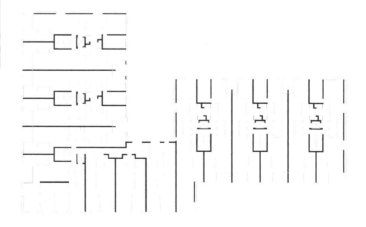

Eichgut
Residences in Winterthur by
Baumschlager Eberle

Concentrated life in the city. Ninety
apartments that are barrier-free, up to 155
square meters in size, and extend from one
side of the building to the other.

Lohbach
Residences in Innsbruck by
Baumschlager Eberle

Seven buildings in an ensemble that
marries aesthetics with economy, ecology,
and barrier-free accessibility.

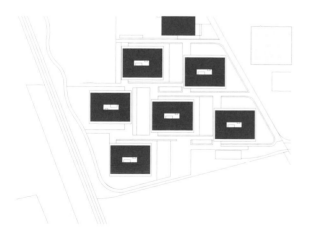

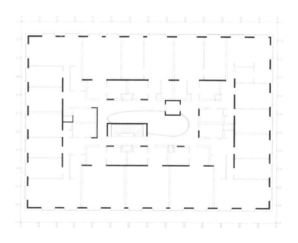

hours per square meter. Barrier-free accessibility, convenience, and ecology are no longer conflicting dimensions.

In 2000 the **Lohbach Residences** were built in Innsbruck for the Neue Heimat Tirol Gemeinnützige Wohnungsbau- und Siedlungsgesellschaft mbH. Seven buildings form a dense residential cluster that offers wonderful views of the surrounding landscape despite the compact configuration. With these cube-like structures, the architects succeeded in squaring the circle: building economically and ecologically with a variety of possible ground plans and a great deal of surrounding greenery. The quality is due to generous moments, despite the compact layout. This can take the form of a panorama or an entrance vestibule that allows daylight to penetrate even into the underground garage. Twenty-six senior-friendly apartments were constructed in Building C, which includes a community room with a kitchen and an office. The personnel here take care of various errands and services ranging from basic supplies, an emergency call system, and private, individual services in "assisted living" spaces. The complex aims to provide assistance for people so they can lead their lives as independently as possible, which might at times mean closing the copper sun protection elements to give the building a bit of variety and liveliness from the outside as well.

STANDARDS DO NOT SOLVE PROBLEMS / INTERVIEW

An interview with Carlo Baumschlager of Baumschlager Eberle
on architects and designing the future

OH **The issue of sustainability is hugely popular today. Are our cities sustainable if this also includes being senior-friendly?**

CB Cities have been around for more than the last twenty years. Their qualities determine whether they are senior-friendly. Collective acceptance is essential here and this involves not only buildings, but also outdoor spaces, streets, and squares. If there is no collective acceptance, however, as displayed by many

Modernist new developments or urban planning decisions, then sustainability is decisively reduced.

OH   **The best design will not function if no one wants it. Are there any particular criteria for acceptance or for qualities that can foster collective acceptance?**

CB   The design has to be able to form a dialog with what already exists and adapt to it. Much of what is built today and which is only related to the object itself, in other words rejects dialog, will prove to be little more than a fad. It will therefore never reflect or support culture. Of course there will be unique instances in certain places, but the majority must address the given context more precisely.

OH   **We have moved from the urban planning aspect to the individual. Yet I do not see any one-family houses that have been built as senior-friendly, let alone barrier-free. What role does barrier-free building play?**

CB   I personally live in a house with an 87-year-old woman, and on a day-to-day basis I witness how the house cannot do what it is actually capable of. When a developer wants a single-family house, he or she is influenced by very different images. Age is not one of them. This has to do with the ideas that influence our society, which again do not include the issue of age. In fact, the opposite is true: you are supposed to remain young. There is too little experience. Becoming old is something relatively new …

OH   **… as a mass phenomenon.**

CB   That as well. We have hospital projects. We are building senior-friendly apartments in collaboration with the Diakonie. Yet everything there, even norms, is based on too little knowledge. There are dozens of books on family living, but nothing on senior-friendly living. There is only very superficial information.

OH   **This is similar to developers who, at least in Germany, have a decisive influence on the market. Products that are promoted as senior-friendly do not make it on the market. Is there a solution for this?**

CB   What developers are producing at the moment has a payback period of thirty years. Age does not play a role here and it has nothing to do with society in the future. The youth of today will inherit only a breakdown, not solutions, which is the opposite of sustainability.

OH   **What can you change, together with the client? What has to change?**

CB   The discussion has to begin with the decision-makers themselves asking what will happen to them when they are older. At least those contributing to the discussion will understand this question, and a completely new perspective will come from a lack of understanding. However, the question about tomorrow is the starting point for the discussion about sustainable action. What we do today should still be valid when we are old. This creates different solutions.

OH   **Can you provide these different solutions?**

CB   The market won't allow it at the moment. It would mean a greater requirement for space, different systems of infrastructure. The additional investment would be relatively low; the added value incomparably high, but no one on the market today anticipates what this added value might be worth. The added value would be clear, but it just has to be made known. Yet if the advantages are not part of the discussion, then no one will see it as an opportunity to give their product a unique advantage. As planners, we work on orders. We might be able to mention that we find certain things disadvantageous, but in general our role is marginal.

OH   **That sounds as if the state should play a role.**

CB   It does already. There are regulations in certain areas. They are most effective when housing subsidies are linked with sustainable developments. The state could choose to grant money only to projects that deal with sustainability. Shaping opinions related to this issue takes time, yet ultimately it is not a political matter. Blindly implementing norms will lead to good business only for a few investors, and low quality for the user.

OH   **In other words, norms will not solve the problem?**

CB   They can't solve it at all. We don't build series, but rather prototypes. And these are geared to context and site. People do not age the same all over. The elderly live in different ways and designers need to respond to this. You can't develop universal norms and pigeonhole the elderly so that they can no longer move freely. Germany is a prime example of the blind application of norms.

OH   **Where are the progressive examples that we can study and perhaps assimilate?**

CB   There are many in the Benelux countries, where they have been addressing the issue of senior-friendly living for quite some time. Or in Sweden where they are researching how to better integrate older people into the city. There are examples that could be studied, but here in Germany it isn't sexy to talk about age. We only have fitness and the youthful elderly.

OH   **Building has to change. But are there also not architects who feel creatively restricted by wide hallways and doors?**

CB   These are not serious problems, but rather formal issues. Actually the discussion should not be about the width of hallways, but should address how proper atmospheric solutions can be achieved. That's what we get paid for.

OH   **To summarize: would you convert you own house?**

CB   Of course, I would install an elevator if necessary. I'll also get old. We all have to address the fact. Here and there, small shoots of change are sprouting. Particularly in the area of hospitals. Hospitals have to be something more than just a machine, they have to care for older people — not methodically, but rather as a service. This is similar to a hotel. It also is not only about older people. It is something everyone else wants, which is partly why things are progressing in this area. Those who pay taxes today will want the service later.

Multigenerational Living: Social Change as Catalyst for New Design Solutions

There is a government-backed campaign to promote the return of the large family, at least in Germany. Multigenerational residences aim to encourage the young and old to live together. Ursula von der Leyen, the Federal Minister for Family, Seniors, Women, and Youth, would like to see them everywhere, in every county, every small community. By 2010 there should be 439 community housing facilities in which the old and the young can learn from and support each other. What is the catch? A type of communal residence, a social cafe?

"Multigenerational housing is a rather soft term," says Christine Degenhart, an architect from Rosenheim and spokesperson for the Barrier-free Building Information Center of the Bavarian Chamber of Architecture (see p. 146). It is first a matter of places to gather during the day where "different groups of people can meet or individuals can find the space for contemplation." Only very few residences provide true communal housing or temporary patchwork families. Initially it will be a matter of taking very small steps at the local level, which aim to provide concrete assistance such as a clothes washing service, computer course, or big brother or sister service. Even these services need to take place within a certain framework — a designed framework. Degenhart believes it is important to have "as much flexibility as possible inside and enough references to the garden outside." Movable partitioning walls divide rooms if someone wants to work and someone else read. Moreover, it is patently obvious that all the buildings are, of course, barrier-free. Good architecture goes beyond that. It is essential to create a "design that is rich in contrast so that older people can immediately orient themselves." The architect goes on to suggest: "It doesn't have to be glaring. On the contrary, the clearer the architecture, the more inclusive it feels."

Yet architecture always remains a shell. It can create possibilities, but cannot level out every social deficit. There are no ideal solutions. Multigenerational residences can develop from family centers or senior meeting places. Such as Haus Heslach which belongs to the Rudolf Schmid and Hermann Schmid Foundation in Stuttgart. It was initially conceived as a nursing home, but developed into a neighborhood shopping center with a supermarket, apartment units, shops, and doctor's offices. There are a wide variety of uses piled on top of one another: at ground level are a public foyer, a bank, and a bakery; above this is the administration level, then the nursing home with direct access to the garden; and the top two floors are for people in need of more care.

The challenge to the Stuttgart-based architects Haag, Haffner, Stroheker was to connect the opposing needs for both quietude and playgrounds and to develop a coherent concept in general. This included soft factors such as atmosphere, a systematic flow of light and clear materials. Not all the residents were happy about details such as the bare ceilings, but overall the building was a great success. It opened in the spring of 2001. Today, it "opens even beyond the neighborhood," explains Carola Haegele who heads the project. Glancing through the building's varied program implies that community can also mean variety, if a social institution is to someday replace the large family.

But this can also work at the private level. In **Gartenpark Höhen-kirchen** located south of Munich, multigeneration residences are being built with gardens, terraces, cellars, and hobby rooms that are advertised by a bright red construction above the parking lot. Grandparents can move here, or even their grandchildren. It is easy to convert the units into independent apartments, because the second-floor levels have their own entrance over an external stairwell, and the plumbing system can accommodate a bathroom and a kitchen on every floor. The multigeneration residences range from 116 to 134 square meters in size and are designed for up to five residents. The units change with each family. The upstairs area can be converted into an independent apartment for the grand-parents with the parents occupying the downstairs level. The units are flexible shells that respond to each different lifestyle with endlessly new constellations.

Architect Tobias de la Ossa has long pursued the idea of a "special type of house that supports true multigeneration living as well as changing residential needs and family structures." The original concept was modified several times while looking for the right client, and the built units are no longer 100 percent barrier-free. The Bayerische Bau und Immobilien GmbH & Co. KG attributes this to high costs. The families were more interested in the division of rooms, heating, alternative energy, or large bathrooms — rather than the inevitable frailness that comes later with age, as the press officer confirms, "Buyers between the ages of thirty and fifty are not thinking about getting old."

Integrated living and barrier-free residences are still a social taboo compared to Scandinavia or Austria. The Federal Ministry's initiative is right on time. Families still care for circa seventy percent of relatives in need of care and, in turn, grandparents regularly raise one third of children. They do not want to be sent to a home. According to one study, circa fifteen percent of older people are considering giving up their apartment or house, whereas many are forced to because only a few households have a floor-level accessible shower, or doors wide enough to accommodate a wheelchair or rollator. In the future, multigeneration residences will need to be more than just daytime meeting centers. They will need to develop into full-fledged residences and, as an institutional replacement for the dying large family, become an essential social bonding element.

Gartenpark Höhenkirchen

Multigeneration Residences near Munich by De la Ossa Architects

Multi-generation residences surrounded by green. Flexible ground floor plans and room divisions. Grandparents upstairs, or children above the carport? Everything is possible in a house that can adapt to the various situations life offers.

GOOD DESIGN IS UNI-VERSAL DESIGN.

JAMES IRVINE

THE FUTURE WILL BE EASY AND COMFORTABLE

"Simplicity" and "Easy to Use" appear on appliances by manufacturers that practice brand management and constantly update a product's distinctive features. Customer loyalty in negative: companies like to have their own user interfaces, expressions, and symbols, even if typical features have long been standardized and are being sold on the international market at the current price.

67—68 Dahm, Markus; Felken, Christian; Klein-Bösing, Marc; Rompel, Gert; Stroick, Roman: "Handyergo: Breite Untersuchung über die Gebrauchstauglichkeit von Handys", in: Reinhard Keil-Slawik, Harald Selke, Gerd Szwillus (ed.): *Mensch & Computer 2004: Allgegenwärtige Interaktion*. Oldenbourg Verlag, Munich, 2004, pp. 75—84; quoted in: http://mc.informatik.uni-hamburg.de/konferenzbaende/mc2004/mc2004_08_dahm_etal.pdf

Complexity continues to be equated with technical progress without developers and engineers really considering the users. And of course researchers claim that, "new, expensive features can only be successful if improvements are made as well." [67] But we still have far to go. Packing more and more functions into ever-smaller appliances has been the objective for many years. Yet not only does the tactile aspect go missing here, but also the relationship to what is in your hand or to its actual function. So as not to be misunderstood: this is not about the old black box conflict, that is solving the mysterious technology inside its more or less swanky casing. The days of the gramophone's belt drive turntable are over. This is, however, about making technology comfortable and designing it to suit the needs of the user — and not vice versa, where people's arms become an extension of the device, or worse, a prisoner of an indecipherable, poorly programmed world of things. More and more functions only make the operating system more difficult to use: "The number of functions increases with every mobile phone generation and selecting them in the menu becomes more and more complicated, nor does the user always know about the new functions and what they do." [68] They identified another weak point that can be easily rectified: small displays offer only a very limited overview of the menu and its structure, which makes it difficult to navigate. And there is another point: economically speaking, optimizing products today means saving money and cutting corners where ever possible — even, unfortunately, if this affects the product's functionality. To save a few centimeters of cable, on/off switches often end up on the back of a product, which is surely inconvenient for the user. This is an important leverage point for future products. Simplicity is often better. Long ago trend researchers coined the term "simplexity," which attempts to combine two opposites: the increasing "complexity" of our technical environment, and the desire for "simplicity." Objects should remain objects, without the technical bombardment.

If technology does in fact develop in three phases, primitive > complex > simple, then the final stage lies ahead. And it will benefit us all. Floor-level drains, Reling systems, and other bathroom innovations show that barrier-free accessibility and emotion are not the opposites they seemed to be. Design that is created allegedly for older people is based on convenience and healthy living and therefore becomes design for everyone: Universal Design. This is accompanied by a multitude of specific improvements, clever placement of switches, logical arrangement of buttons, and easy to understand function menus. Universal Design is a trend that is not a trend. It is about investing in a future that does not end at sixty years of age. We are getting older and older — architecture and design must adapt, or better still radically simplify our environment. This requires rethinking our perspectives. Age is first and foremost a social construction. Findings gathered from age research on the domestic environment, mobility, communication, and so on, will find their way into new products. The guidelines for tomorrow's design will change from farther and faster, to wider and simpler, more convenient and easier. Intuitive devices will help users operate the basic functions with ease. There is also a great need for consultation here, as with the evaluation of the results of technology. At the same time, services have an opportunity to create new markets.

We are on the threshold of a new age that, for the first time since the onset of mass production, focuses once again on customers and their needs as well as their desire to live in a barrier-free world with devices that can be operated intuitively. We are standing before the revolution of our product culture, which is no longer forced to promote achievements in technology, but understands it as a basis that is self-evident, as an aid and a service. The future promises to be more comfortable. But first, many barriers have to be removed — especially those in our minds.

APPENDIX

The Principles of Universal Design

Copyright 1997 NC State University, The Center for Universal Design

----

PRINCIPLE 1:

Equitable Use
The design is useful and marketable to people with
diverse abilities.

Guidelines:
· Provide the same means of use for all users: identical whenever
  possible; equivalent when not.
· Avoid segregating or stigmatizing any users.
· Provisions for privacy, security, and safety should be equally
  available to all users.
· Make the design appealing to all users.

PRINCIPLE 2:

Flexibility in Use
The design accommodates a wide range of
individual preferences and abilities.

Guidelines:
· Provide choice in methods of use.
· Accommodate right- or left-handed access and use.
· Facilitate the user's accuracy and precision.
· Provide adaptability to the user's pace.

PRINCIPLE 3:

Simple and Intuitive Use
Use of the design is easy to understand, regardless
of the user's experience, knowledge, language skills, or
current concentration level.

Guidelines:
· Eliminate unnecessary complexity.
· Be consistent with user expectations and intuition.
· Accommodate a wide range of literacy and language skills.
· Arrange information consistent with its importance.
· Provide effective prompting and feedback during and after task
  completion.

PRINCIPLE 4:

Perceptible Information
The design communicates necessary information effectively to the user, regardless of ambient conditions or the user's sensory abilities.

Guidelines:
· Use different modes (pictorial, verbal, tactile) for redundant presentation of essential information.
· Provide adequate contrast between essential information and its surroundings.
· Maximize "legibility" of essential information.
· Differentiate elements in ways that can be described (i.e., make it easy to give instructions or directions).
· Provide compatibility with a variety of techniques or devices used by people with sensory limitations.

PRINCIPLE 5:

Tolerance for Error
The design minimizes hazards and the adverse consequences of accidental or unintended actions.

Guidelines:
· Arrange elements to minimize hazards and errors: most used elements, most accessible; hazardous elements eliminated, isolated, or shielded.
· Provide warnings of hazards and errors.
· Provide fail safe features.
· Discourage unconscious action in tasks that require vigilance.

PRINCIPLE 6:

Low Physical Effort
The design can be used efficiently and comfortably and with a minimum of fatigue.

Guidelines:
· Allow user to maintain a neutral body position.
· Use reasonable operating forces.
· Minimize repetitive actions.
· Minimize sustained physical effort.

PRINCIPLE 7:

Size and Space for Approach and Use
Appropriate size and space is provided for approach, reach, manipulation, and use regardless of user's body size, posture, or mobility.

Guidelines:

· Provide a clear line of sight to important elements for any seated or standing user.
· Make reach to all components comfortable for any seated or standing user.
· Accommodate variations in hand and grip size.
· Provide adequate space for the use of assistive devices or personal assistance.

Please note that the Principles of Universal Design address only universally usable design, while the practice of design involves more than consideration for usability. Designers must also incorporate other considerations such as economic, engineering, cultural, gender, and environmental concerns in their design processes. These Principles offer designers guidance to better integrate features that meet the needs of as many users as possible.

Abbreviations

ADF	(Accessibility Design Foundation)
AIGA	(American Institute of Graphic Arts)
ARPANET	(Advanced Research Projects Agency Network)
BAGSO	(Bundesarbeitsgemeinschaft der Senioren-Organisationen e. V. [German National Association of Senior Citizen's Organizations])
DIMR	(Deutsches Institut für Menschenrechte [German Institute for Human Rights])
ESPA	(Elderly Service Providers Association)
GRP	(Generation Research Program, LMU Munich)
IMP	(Interface Messaging Processor)
METI	(Ministry for Economy, Trade and Industry)
PDA	(Personal Digital Assistant)
PM	(Personal Mobility)
RFID	(Radio Frequency Identification)
RNID	(Royal National Institute for the Deaf)
sentha	(Seniorengerechte Technik im häuslichen Alltag [Senior-friendly Technology in the Everyday Household])
NIA	(National Institute on Aging)
TAS	(Tourist Assistance System for barrier-free Access)
Whoopies	(Well-off older people)

Bibliography

Altes, schrumpfendes Europa. Die Herausforderung des demographischen Wandels (Old shrinking Europe. The challenge of demographic change). Bertelsmann Stiftung seminar 2006. http://www.bertelsmann-stiftung.de/bst/de/media/xcms_bst_dms_16305_16306_2.pdf

Barrierefreies und Integriertes Wohnen. Forschungsbericht zur Nachuntersuchung ausgewählter Projekte aus Modellvorhaben und Landeswettbewerb (Barrier-free accessibility and integrated living. Research report on the study of selected projects from planned models and the national competition). Oberste Baubehörde im Bayerischen Staatsministerium des Inneren (Supreme building authority of the Bavarian State Ministry of the Interior) (ed.): (Materialien zum Wohnungsbau [Materials on residential construction]). Munich, 2006. http://www.experimenteller-wohnungsbau.bayern.de/pdf/bfw-brosch.pdf

Beschwerdepool für ältere Verbraucher. Ergebnisse der Befragung zum Thema Verpackungen (Grievance platform for older consumers on the subject of packaging) http://www.bagso.de/fileadmin/Verbraucherforum/Verpackungen_01.pdf

Braun, Reiner; Pfeiffer, Ulrich: *Wohnflächennachfrage in Deutschland* (Living space requirements in Germany). Empirica, Berlin, 2005, p. 4. http://www.empirica-institut.de/kufa/empi123rb.pdf

Burckhardt, Lucius: "Design ist unsichtbar" (Design is invisible). In: *Design ist unsichtbar*. Edited by Helmut Gsöllpointer, Angela Hareiter and Laurids Ortner. Österreichisches Institut für Visuelle Gestaltung (The Austrian Institute for Visual Design). Löcker, Vienna, 1981, pp. 13—20.

Dahm, Markus; Felken, Christian; Klein-Bösing, Marc; Rompel, Gert; Stroick, Roman: "Handy ERGO: Breite Untersuchung über die Gebrauchstauglichkeit von Handys" (Mobile phone ergo: a comprehensive study on the usability of mobile phones), in: *Mensch & Computer 2004: Allgegenwärtige Interaktion* (Ubiquitous interaction). Edited by Reinhard Keil-Slawik, Harald Selke and Gerd Szwillus. Oldenbourg Verlag, Munich, 2004, pp. 75—84; quoted in: http://mc.informatik.uni-hamburg.de/konferenzbaende/mc2004/mc2004_08_dahm_etal.pdf

Degenhart, Christine: *Freiraum. Das Haus fürs Leben, frei von Barrieren* (Open space. The house of a lifetime, free of barriers). Landkreis Rosenheim (ed.), 2000; see also: http://www.byak-barrierefrei.de/byak-barrfrei_publikationen.htm

Gerling, Vera; Conrad, Harald: *Wirtschaftskraft Alter in Japan*. Handlungsfelder und Strategien (The economic power of the elderly in Japan. Fields of action and strategies). Expertise commissioned by the Bundesministerium für Familie, Senioren, Frauen und Jugend (Minister of family, seniors, women, and youth), 2002. As PDF: http://www.ffg.uni-dortmund.de/medien/publikationen/Expertise%20Japanischer%20Silbermarkt.pdf

Gruss, Peter (ed.): *Die Zukunft des Alterns*. Die Antwort der Wissenschaft (The future of aging. The answer offered by science). Beck, Munich, 2007.

Gsöllpointer, Helmut; Hareiter, Angela; Ortner, Laurids (eds.): *Design ist unsichtbar*. Österreichisches Institut für Visuelle Gestaltung (The Austrian Institute for Visual Design). Löcker, Vienna, 1981.

Häußermann, Hartmut: "Altern in der Stadt" (Aging in the city). In: *Wohnen im Alter. Visionen, Realitäten, Erfahrungen* (Senior living. Visions, reality, experience). Oberste Baubehörde im Bayerischen des Inneren (Supreme building authority of the Bavarian State Ministry of the Interior) (ed.): Documentation of the seminar on February 21, 2006, pp. 21—40; here p. 22.

Hundert wird bald jeder (Soon we will all reach 100). Press report by the Max Planck Gesellschaft, September 27, 2007. http://www.mpg.de/bilderBerichteDokumente/dokumentation/pressemitteilungen/2007/pressemitteilung200709272/genPDF.pdf

Krings-Heckemeier, Marie-Therese: *Das silberne Zeitalter — Wie wir den Wandel zu einer Gesellschaft der erweiterten Lebensspannen bewältigen können* (The silver age — how we can make the shift to a society of extended life spans). Empirica, Berlin, 2007. http://www.empirica-institut.de/kufa/empi155mtk.pdf

Von Kuehnheim, Haug: "Gib Gas, Alter!" In: *DIE ZEIT* no. 11, March 9 2006. http://www.zeit.de/2006/11/Rentner_11

Kyôyo-Hin Foundation (2001): *Kyôyo-Hin Foundation*, Japan. www.kyoyohin.org; PDF at: http://www.kyoyohin.org/09_foreign/English_ver.pdf

Lihotzky, Grete: "Rationalization in the Household." In: Anton Kaes, Martin Jay, and Edward Dimendberg (eds.): *The Weimar Republic Sourcebook*, University of California, 1994, pp. 462—5. First published as "Rationalisierung im Haushalt." In: *Das Neue Frankfurt*, no. 5 (1926—1927), pp. 120—3.

Mitchell, William J.: *City of Bits. Space, Place and the Infobahn*. MIT Press, Cambridge, MA, 1996.

Moggridge, Bill: *Designing Interactions*. MIT Press, Cambridge, MA, 2007.

Muthesius, Hermann: "Maschinenarbeit" (Machine work). In: *Technische Abende im Zentralinstitut für Erziehung und Unterricht* (Technical evenings at the Central Institute for Education and Schooling) 4/1917. E. S. Mittler und Sohn, Königliche Hofbuchhandlung. Berlin, 1917, pp. 10—15.

Nutzerfreundliche Produkte. Leicht bedienbar und Generationengerecht (User-friendly products. Easy to use for all generations) BAGSO; http://www.bagso.de/fileadmin/Aktuell/Brosch_re_Nutzerfreundliche_Produkte.pdf

Pollack, Karin: "Was ist eigentlich RFID?" (What actually is RFID?) *brand eins* 1/2005. http://www.brandeins.de/home/inhalt_detail.asp?id=1599&MenuID=130&MagID=59&sid=su84150124831740210&umenuid=1
Scheytt, Stefan: "Woopies. Sie haben Geld. Sie haben Zeit. Und alte Menschen können noch eine Menge brauchen." (Whoopies. They have money. They have time. And seniors still need a lot of things). *brand eins* 9/2005. http://www.brandeins.de/ximages/24315_100diealte.pdf

Schmidt-Ruhland, Karin (ed.): *Pack ein — pack aus — pack zu. Neue Verpackungen für Alt und Jung* (Pack in — pack out — take hold. New packaging for the old and young). Berlin University of the Arts, 2006.

Schwarz, Dietrich: "Sustainable Design." In: *Werkbundsiedlung Wiesenfeld*. Volume 5. (Werkbundtage 2. Material und Technik). Munich, 2007, pp. 89—97.

Schweitzer, Hanne: *Kommentar zum 5. Altenbericht der Bundesregierung* (Commentary on the federal government's fifth age report). Büro gegen Altersdiskriminierung e. V., 3.10.2006. http://www.altersdiskriminierung.de/themen/artikel.php?id=1576

Senior Finance. BBE-Branchenreport. Cologne, 2006. http://www.bbeberatung.com/de/hkg/index.php?/de/pressedienst/news/seniorfinance.php

Streitz, Norbert A.; Tandler, Peter; Müller-Tomfelde, Christian; Konomi, Shin'ichi: "Roomware. Towards the Next Generation of Human-Computer Interaction based on an Integrated Design of Real and Virtual Worlds." In: Carroll, John M. (ed.): *Human-Computer Interaction in the New Millennium*, Addison-Wesley, London, 2001, pp. 553—78.

Vierter Altenbericht zur Lage der älteren Generation in der Bundesrepublik Deutschland (The fourth age report on the condition of older generations in Federal Republic of Germany): *Risiken, Lebensqualität und Versorgung Hochaltriger — unter besonderer Berücksichtigung Erkrankungen* (Risks, quality of life and the care of the elderly — with special attention given to dementia diseases), 2004. http://www.bmfsfj.de/Kategorien/Forschungsnetz/forschungsberichte,did=18370

Wohnen im Alter. Visionen, Realitäten, Erfahrungen (The senior life. Visions, reality, experience). Oberste Baubehörde im Bayerischen Staatsministerium des Inneren (Supreme Building Authority of the Bavarian State Ministry of the Interior) (ed.): Documentation of the seminar on February 21, 2006. http://www.innenministerium.bayern.de/imperia/md/content/stmi/bauen/wohnungswesen/aktuell/broschueretagung-internet.pdf

Yoshikazu, Goto (2002): "Aging Populations, New Business Opportunities and New Business Models Developed in Japan." In: *Journal of Japanese Trade & Industry*, May/June 2002, pp. 24—7.

*   All quotes in this publication taken from German sources were translated by Laura Bruce.

Photo Credits

Imprint

Translation from German into English: Laura Bruce, Berlin
English Copy Editing: Lucinda Byatt, Edinburgh

Library of Congress Control Number: 2008929013

Bibliographic information published by the German
National Library
The German National Library lists this publication in the
Deutsche Nationalbibliografie; detailed bibliographic data
are available on the Internet at http://dnb.d-nb.de.

This book is also available in a German language edition
(ISBN 978-3-7643-8717-4).

© 2008 Birkhäuser Verlag AG
Basel · Boston · Berlin
P.O. Box 133, CH-4010 Basel, Switzerland
Part of Springer Science+Business Media

Printed on acid-free paper produced from chlorine-free
pulp. TCF ∞

Layout: Nadine Rinderer, Basel

Printed in Germany

ISBN: 978-3-7643-8718-1

9 8 7 6 5 4 3 2 1   www.birkhauser.ch